Slogans

compiled by
Nigel Rees

London
GEORGE ALLEN & UNWIN
Boston   Sydney

George Allen & Unwin (Publishers) Ltd
40 Museum Street, London WC1A 1LU

First published in 1982

British Library Cataloguing in Publication Data

Rees, Nigel
    Slogans.
1. Slogans
I. Title
659.13   HF5828
ISBN 0-04-827064-4

Designed by Stonecastle Graphics,
Tunbridge Wells, Kent

Set in 10 on 12pt VIP Melior
by Computape (Pickering) Ltd

Printed in Great Britain
by Fakenham Press Ltd, Fakenham, Norfolk

CONTENTS

All over London the lights flickered in and out, calling on the public to save its body and purse . . . Whatever you're doing, stop it and do something else! Whatever you're buying, pause and buy something different! Be hectored into health and prosperity! Never let up! Never go to sleep! If once you are satisfied, all our wheels will run down. Keep going – and if you can't, Try Nutrax for Nerves!

Dorothy L. Sayers,
Murder Must Advertise

What passes for culture in my head is really a bunch of commercials.

Kurt Vonnegut junior

PREFACE

This is the age of the slogan. They leap out at us from countless billboards, TV screens, T-shirts, bumper stickers and buttons. Politicians and minorities hector us with them; polishers of diamonds, makers of movies and slicers of bread use them to nudge and cajole. We even wear and bear slogans ourselves to proclaim our beliefs and sexual preferences. They show what we stand for and what we will not stand for.

There is much feeble-minded puffery. There is also much that is lively, arresting and entertaining. Only occasionally do slogans achieve excellence or memorability or touch a popular chord. This book sets out to record a thousand or so notable examples, good and bad.

What is a slogan? Richard Usborne defined it as 'a form of words for which memorability has been bought'. Indeed, few of the following phrases would have arisen without bidding. Unlike those phrases from entertainment which spontaneously catch on, the success of these slogans has been engineered and encouraged. In some cases, vast sums of money have been spent to keep them before the public. They rarely contain universal truths or profound insights. They may not be true at all. The distance between a copywriter's fancy and reality can be infinite.

The common denominator is that all these phrases *promote* a product, a cause or an idea.

In strict advertising parlance, the slogan is the phrase which comes at the end of the ad and encapsulates the message. It has been said that it should never comprise more than seven words. The advertiser's devout wish is that the phrase will then continue to buzz around the consumer's head, further enforcing the message. There are, in addition, certain advertising phrases which are generally regarded as slogans because they are associated with specific products.

Good To The Last Drop
Does She ... Or Doesn't She?
It Beats As It Sweeps As It Cleans

These phrases have the *power* of slogans even if they are not self-sufficient. The days are long gone when a perfect slogan was supposed to name and define a product as well as promising some benefit.

In short, this book is devoted to slogans in the broadest sense. It includes phrases that stand out from advertising, political campaigns or promotions with a social purpose, and also mottoes and catchwords which carry the force of full-blooded slogans.

In trying to discover when and where these phrases were first used, together with some indication of how and by whom they were created, I was frequently told that their origins had been lost in the mists of time. Only a few commercial or political organisations have assembled archives recording their promotional activities. Even among those which have, few have bothered to record specifically who coined the phrases which have helped give enduring success or fame to their products.

There are some people in advertising who feel that this is only proper. One creative chief warned: 'If you are going to try and credit individuals with slogans, you are inevitably going to upset an awful lot of people. Slogans tend to evolve by some strange form of osmosis and normally more than one person can genuinely lay claim to having made a contribution.' Indeed, in advertising more than most professions 'success has a hundred fathers and failure is an orphan'. Nevertheless, when it has been possible to get somewhere near the truth it has been thought worthwhile to point a finger.

A further complication is that advertising agencies are for ever splitting up, regrouping under ever more peculiar names – and occasionally they lose accounts in sudden-death situations which erase memories of even the proudest achievements.

All this applies equally, if not more, to slogans carrying a social or political message. These often arise out of a popular mood and are snapped up before anyone has had time to record how they were formulated.

So, inevitably, much of the information here gathered is incomplete. Corrections and suggestions for future editions will be warmly welcomed.

Slogans can be either sharp or blunt instruments, even if it is hard to measure what slogans do to our minds by simplifying issues and purveying propaganda or what they do to our language by relying so heavily on puns, alliteration, rhythm and balance. This book is a celebration of slogans, but one tempered with a certain irreverence. Occasional examples have been included of the way in which slogans have been alluded to or maltreated in other contexts. If manufacturers or even copywriters recoil, they should console themselves with the knowledge that they have contributed something to the language.

At one time everybody seemed to have a slogan. The crisp phrase was refreshing after the torrents of verbiage that characterised early advertising. Now, whether in press ads or on TV, there is a greater emphasis on the visual. One agency creative director comments:

'Slogans have to be brilliant to work, and actually say something rather than merely boast. If all that can be said is a bit of clever puff, we'd rather do without.'

What, then, makes a successful slogan? There is only one test – whether it promotes the product or cause effectively. **Votes For Women** is not notably witty but it achieved its purpose. On the other hand, there are plenty of phrases which have 'caught on' but which have failed to promote the product or the cause.

Now the time has come to 'run this book up the flagpole and see if anyone salutes it' and to 'put it out on the porch and see if the cat eats it' – to use those phrases beloved of advertising folk. If the collective noun for the phrases that follow is a 'boast' of slogans, let the boasting begin.

London, 1982

NOTE

'US' or 'UK' signifies no more than the country of origin;

'from 1963' – slogan first used in that year;

'current 1963' – documentary evidence is available of the slogan in use that year, though it probably arose earlier;

'quoted 1963' – means no more than that; the slogan was most likely coined or current well before.

Names of sources are given in parentheses; fuller reference is given in the Acknowledgements (p. 168).

I'D LOVE A BEER[*]

The Beer That Made Milwaukee Famous Schlitz; US, from *c.*
1895. The Jos. Schlitz Brewing Company has its roots in an
operation begun in Milwaukee in 1849. By 1871, the year of the
great Chicago fire, it was a thriving concern. The fire left Chicago
thirsty. The city was desperately short of drinking water and its
breweries had virtually been destroyed. So Joseph Schlitz floated a
shipload of beer down Lake Michigan to refresh his parched
neighbours. They liked and remembered the Milwaukee beer long
after the crisis passed. It is not known who coined the phrase but
this is the incident which led to it. The slogan was incorporated in a
label and registered in 1895, and has been in use ever since.

Claude C. Hopkins, one of advertising's immortals, was once
engaged on a campaign for Schlitz. He was taken on a tour of the
brewery to give him ideas. He saw the malt and the hops but his
enthusiasm for the steam bath, in which the bottles were washed
before being filled with beer, was unbounded. As the client was at
pains to point out, this method was standard in all breweries, but
Hopkins realised that the point had never been used in ads before.
Hence: **Our Bottles Are Washed With Live Steam**.

THE BEER THAT MADE MILWAUKEE FAMOUS

A Double Diamond Works Wonders Double Diamond; UK, from
1952. Double alliteration may have something to do with it, but it
was surely the singing of this slogan to the tune of 'There's a Hole in
my Bucket' that made it one of the best known of all beer slogans. In
1971, a visiting American copywriter, Ros Levenstein, came up
with the phrase **I'm Only Here For The Beer**, which has passed into
the language as an inconsequential catchphrase.

[*]A generic campaign in New Zealand (current 1981) tried to woo people
away from wine-drinking with this slogan.

For An A1 Nation Beer Is Best   Brewers Society; UK, from 1933.
Part of a campaign to restore the pub's status as a social centre and
to 'publicize the goodness of beer produced from prime barley and
full-flavoured hops':

> On working days
>   or holidays
> On dismal days
>   or jolly days –
> Beer is best.

The temperance variant was: 'Beer is best – left alone'.

Gone For A Burton   Folk-memory suggests that this phrase was originally used in the UK prior to the Second World War to promote a Bass brew known in the trade as 'a Burton' (though, in fact, several ales are brewed in Burton-upon-Trent). However, research has failed to turn up more positive proof. Early in the war, the phrase was adopted as an idiom to describe what had happened to a missing person, presumed dead, especially in the RAF.

Great Stuff This Bass!   Bass; UK, current 1928. A character called 'Bill Sticker' was shown in ads plastering this slogan in various unlikely places.

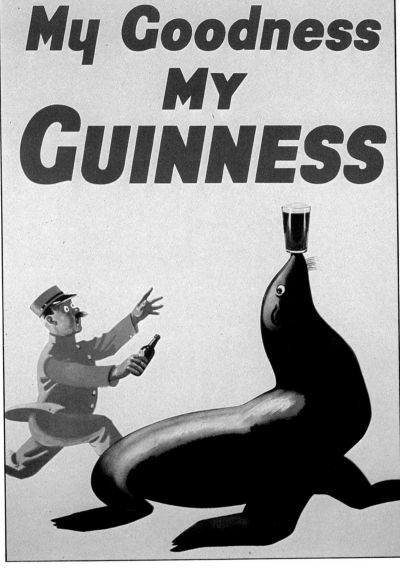

Guinness Is Good For You   Guinness; UK, from 1929. After 170 years without advertising, Arthur Guinness Son & Company decided to call in the image-makers. Oswald Greene at S. H. Benson initiated some consumer research (unusual in those days) into why people were drinking Guinness. 'We spent an awful lot of time in an awful lot of pubs,' recalled a colleague. Wherever they went they found that people thought Guinness did them good. Greene spotted the potential in this approach, though the slogan was nearly rejected as being too ordinary and not clever enough. The claim also conflicts with the fact that most drinkers drink for social reasons rather than for health.

The slogan has been revived only once since being discontinued *c.* 1941 because claims for the health-giving powers of alcohol are frowned upon nowadays. The Advertising Standards Authority says that, technically, Guinness has never fallen foul of it because the 'Good For You' claim has not been made during the Authority's existence, adding: 'It is not certain it would offend.'

There is a story Guinness like to tell about the man who questioned the amount of money they spend each year telling him to drink the stuff. 'The only reason I drink Guinness', he said, 'is because it's good for me.'

Ask any British person to give an example of an advertising slogan and he is more than likely to say 'Guinness is good for you'. It is etched on the national consciousness to such an extent that although the slogan has not been used since 1963 people remember it as though they saw it yesterday.

Guinness Gives You Strength first appeared in 1929 as 'Guinness Is So Strengthening' and ran until 1959. It achieved its most memorable form in the 1934 poster by John Gilroy which shows a man carrying an iron girder on his fingertips.

As for **My Goodness, My Guinness**, Dicky Richards, Benson's art director, got the idea of a zoo-keeper chasing a sealion which had stolen his Guinness after he had paid a visit to the circus at Olympia. This led to a whole menagerie of animals being associated with the product between 1935 and 1958 – ostriches, lions, kinkajous and, above all, toucans. These last emerged as the brainchild of Dorothy L. Sayers, the novelist, who was then a copywriter at Benson's:

If he can say as you can
Guinness is good for you
How grand to be a Toucan
Just think what Toucan do

> If he can say as you can
> Guinness is good for you,
> How grand to be a Toucan
> Just think what Toucan do.

Give Him/'Em A Guinness marked the removal to J. Walter Thompson of the Guinness account in 1969. Ironically, the form of the slogan had been used by Benson's many years previously to promote Bovril. It was followed by **7 Million Every Day And Still Going Down** in 1971 (which seems quite modest beside the 1955 Coca-Cola jingle **Fifty Million Times A Day**) and the pointed line **I've Never Tried It Because I Don't Like It** in 1973. In addition, there was a string of puns: **Tall, Dark And Have Some**; **Cool, Calm And Collect It**; **Hop Squash**; **Pint Sighs**; and, in Jubilee Year, **We've Poured Through The Reign**. None of these quite rose to the depths, however, of the old Benson's line, **Pour Encourager Les Huîtres**.

Harp Puts Out The Fire   Harp Lager; UK, from *c.* 1976. Keith Ravenscroft, who coined the phrase at Ayer Barker, is surprised that no one remarked on the detumescent promise inherent in this otherwise successful slogan.

Heineken. Refreshes the parts other beers cannot reach.

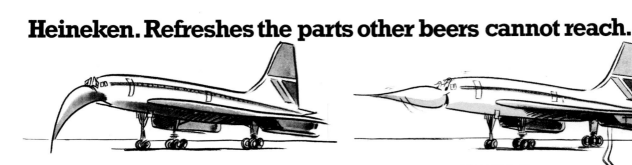

Heineken Refreshes The Parts Other Beers Cannot Reach
Heineken Lager; UK, from 1975. 'I wrote the slogan,' says Terry
Lovelock, 'during December 1974 at 3 a.m. at the Hotel Marmounia
in Marrakesh. After eight weeks of incubation with the agency
(Collett, Dickenson, Pearce), it was really a brainstorm. No other
lines were written. The trip was to refresh the brain. Expensive, but
it worked.' The slogan has always been linked to amusing visuals –
the 'droop-snoot' of Concorde raised by an infusion of the brew; a
piano tuner's ears sharpened; or a policeman's toes refreshed.
There has also been a strong topical element: when Chia-Chia, a
panda from the London Zoo, was sent off in 1981 to mate with
Ling-Ling in Washington, a full-page press ad merely said 'Good
Luck Chia-Chia from Heineken', the slogan being understood.

This kind of claim is allowed under the British Code of
Advertising Practice, Section 4.2.3.: 'Obvious untruths or exagger-
ations, intended to catch the eye or amuse, are permissible
provided that they are clearly to be seen as humorous or hyperbolic
and are not likely to be understood as making literal claims for the
advertised product.'

How Do You Feel? I Feel Like A Toohey's Toohey's beer;
Australia, current 1980.

It Looks Good, Tastes Good And, By Golly, It *Does* You Good
Mackeson; UK, current 1950s. The notion of beer being 'good for
you' – a key element in Guinness advertising over the years – was
eroded by the rise of consumer and advertising watchdogs. As if to
avoid any conflict with the massed ranks of such people, Mackeson
revived the slogan in 1981 but substituted a row of dots after 'By
Golly . . .'.

It's What Your Right Arm's For Courage Tavern; UK, current
1972. Although this line became a popular catchphrase it risks
being applied to rival products, whereas the earlier **Take Courage**
(current 1966) clearly does not.

Probably The Best Lager In The World Carlsberg; UK, from 1973.
Even were it not intoned by Orson Welles in the TV ads, the
'probably' inserted into this hyperbole would still fascinate.

AIRLINES

A problem all airlines share is in projecting a distinct image when the nature of the service they offer can differ only in minor respects. They also seem bound to pretend that being thrust through the air at 39,000 feet, in a cramped metal tube, is somehow a glamorous, life-enhancing experience. Here the reassuring slogans and corporate tags are brought into play, though putting **Say Hello To A Brand New World** on the emergency exit of a Pan Am jet hardly puts you at ease, and Air Siam's **We Serve You Better – Not Just A Slogan: A Commitment** seems unduly apologetic.

How far have the airlines succeeded in differentiating themselves? These are the slogans, old and new. To which companies do they apply? (The answers are on page 18.)

1 **I'm Margie. Fly Me**
2 **You're Going To Like Us**
3 **A Great Way To Fly**
4 **We Fly The World The Way The World Wants To Fly**
5 **The End Of The Plain Plane**
6 **Ready When You Are**
7 **The Airline Run By Professionals**
8 **We Never Forget You Have A Choice**
9 **We'll Take *More* Care Of You**
10 **No. 1 In Europe**
11 **When You Got It, Flaunt It**
12 **Fly The Friendly Skies Of Your Land**
13 **Doing What We Do Best**
14 **We Have To Earn Our Wings Every Day**
15 **The Wings Of Man**
16 **We Really Move Our Tails For You**

ANSWERS

1   National Airlines; US, current c. 1971. The campaign, also using **I'm Going To Fly You Like You've Never Been Flown Before**, aroused the ire of feminist groups. Later, Wall's Sausages sent up the slogan with **I'm Meaty, Fry Me**.

2   TWA; US, current 1980. In 1967, when TWA hinted that they might be on the point of quitting their New York agency, Foote, Cone & Belding saved its bacon by slipping over to California and buying sole rights to the Jim Webb song 'Up, Up and Away'. They proceeded to incorporate this in the airline's ads as **Up, Up And Away With TWA**.

3   Singapore Airlines; US, current 1980.

4   Pan Am; US, current 1980.

5   Braniff; US, from 1965. Braniff planes were painted in bright colours and the hostesses dressed in Pucci outfits.

6   Delta; US, from 1968.

7   Delta is, too.

8   British Caledonian; UK, current 1981.

9   British Airways; UK, current 1976. Originally **BOAC Takes Good Care Of You (All Over The World)** and adapted when the airline changed its name. Japan Air Lines began to say they would take **Good Care Of You, Too** but were persuaded to drop the line, although they had used **Love At First Flight** a dozen years before BOAC took up the slogan (Nicholl). In its time, BA has ranged from the patriotic **Fly The Flag** to **Try A Little VC 10derness**.

10 British European Airways (before being incorporated with BOAC in BA).

11 Braniff; US, current 1969. Used on ads featuring celebrities like Sonny Liston, Andy Warhol and Joe Namath. Perhaps the line was acquired from the 1967 Mel Brooks movie *The Producers*, where it appears as 'If you got it, baby, flaunt it'.

12 United; US, from 1973. Also **Fly The Friendly Skies Of United**.

13 American Airlines; US, current 1980.

14 Eastern Airlines; US, current 1980.

15 Eastern, too.

16 Continental; US, current 1975. In that year some of the airline's stewardesses threatened to sue over the 'bad taste' it had shown in selecting this slogan.

I'm Margie. Fly me.

Delta is ready when you are

British airways
We'll take more care of you

"Another big apple, ma'am?"

Fly the friendly skies of United.
Call your Travel Agent.

EASTERN
WE HAVE TO EARN OUR WINGS EVERY DAY.

BLACK POWER

The civil rights struggle in the United States as proclaimed through its slogans:

Abolition! Originally a cry of the white colonists, c. 1765, demanding the repeal of the British Stamp Act. After repeal in 1766, it was widely applied to the abolition of slavery.

Amistad! In 1839, fifty-four slaves aboard the Spanish schooner *Amistad* on a voyage from Cuba murdered the captain and three crew members. They ordered the remaining crew to sail to Africa. Instead, they found themselves taken to Long Island and imprisoned. Subsequently, they were freed and returned to Africa. The cry was taken up by militants in the 1960s.

Black Is Beautiful Martin Luther King junior launched a poster campaign round this slogan in 1967 but Stokely Carmichael had used the phrase at a Memphis civil rights rally in 1966. It may have its origins in The Song of Solomon 1:1: 'I am black, but comely.'

Black Power An all-purpose slogan encompassing just about anything that people want it to mean, from simple pride in the black race to a threat of violence. The Harlem Congressman Adam Clayton Powell junior said in a baccalaureate address at Howard University in May 1966: 'To demand these God-given rights is to seek black power – what I call audacious power – the power to build black institutions of splendid achievement.' On 6 June, James Meredith, the first black to integrate the University of Mississippi (in 1962), was shot and wounded during a civil rights march. Stokely Carmichael, heading the Student Non-violent Coordinating Committee, continued the march, during which his contingent first used the shout. Carmichael used the phrase in a speech at Greenwood, Mississippi, the same month. It was also adopted as a slogan by the Congress for Racial Equality. However, the notion was not new in the 1960s. Langston Hughes had written in *Simple Takes a Wife* (1953): 'Negro blood is so powerful – because just *one* drop of black blood makes a coloured man – *one* drop – you are a Negro! ... Black is powerful.' (Bartlett/Flexner/Safire)

Burn, Baby, Burn! A black extremists' slogan following the August 1965 riots in the Watts district of Los Angeles when thirty-four people were killed and entire blocks burned down.

Emancipation! The Fugitive Slave Act of 1850 attempted to stop people helping escaped slaves and allowed owners to pursue them even into free states. Abolitionists adopted the cry to reflect a broader concern beyond a straightforward abolition of slavery.

Freedom Now! In the early 1960s, a black litany went:

Q. What do you want?
A. Freedom!
Q. Let me hear it again – what do you want?
A. Freedom!
Q. When do you want it?
A. Now!

This format may have arisen from a petition delivered to Governor George Wallace of Alabama in March 1965. On this occasion Martin Luther King junior and other civil rights leaders led some 3,000 people in a 50-mile march from Selma to Montgomery. The petition began: 'We have come to you, the Governor of Alabama, to declare that we must have our freedom now. We must have the right to vote; we must have equal protection of the law, and an end to police brutality.'

Jim Crow [clap, clap] Must Go! The phrase 'Jim Crow' became common in the 1880s but goes back to the 1730s when blacks were first called 'crows'. By 1835 'Jim Crow' or 'Jim Crowism' meant segregation. Hence the early 1960s street chant.

Power To The People Shouted with clenched fist raised – a slogan of the Black Panther movement and publicised as such by its leader, Bobby Seale, in Oakland, California, July 1969. Also used by other dissident groups, as illustrated by Eldridge Cleaver: 'We say "All Power to the People" – Black Power for Black People, White Power for White People, Brown Power for Brown People, Red Power for Red People, and X Power for any group we've left out.' It was this somewhat generalised view of 'People Power' that John Lennon appeared to promote in the 1971 song 'Power to the People (Right on!)'.

Ten Acres And A Mule were what was sought by slaves from 1862 onwards. They thought that their masters' plantations would be divided up to their benefit after the Civil War. However, this escalated to **Forty Acres And A Mule** when, in January 1865, General Sherman stated that 'Every family shall have a plot of not more than forty acres of tillable ground' – a promise which had nothing to do with the Federal government. Consequently, this

Reconstruction slogan dwindled to **Three Acres And A Cow**. *This* phrase had originated in John Stuart Mill's *Principles of Political Economy* (1848) – 'When the land is cultivated entirely by the spade and no horses are kept, a cow is kept for every three acres of land.' Jesse Collings (1831–1920), a henchman of Joseph Chamberlain in the 1880s, proposed that every smallholder in the UK should have these things. He was an advocate of radical agrarian policies and the smallholding movement. He became known as 'Three Acres And A Cow Collings'. (Noel Coward once described Edith, Osbert and Sacheverell Sitwell as 'two wiseacres and a cow'.)

We Shall Overcome From a song that became the civil rights anthem of the early 1960s. It originated in pre-Civil-War times, was adapted as a Baptist hymn called 'I'll Overcome Some Day', *c.* 1900, by C. Albert Hindley, and first became famous when sung by black workers on a picket line in Charleston, South Carolina, 1946. Pete Seeger and others added verses.

Oh, deep in my heart, I know that I do believe,
We shall overcome some day.

In the Spanish Civil War a Republican chant was ¡**Venceremos**! which means the same thing.

Stokely Carmichael

HEY! WHY DON'T WE SAY...

Lurking in almost every copywriter's mind is a streak of icono-clasm and bad taste which gets sublimated in the telling of jokes about the lines they would love to have written about the products if only they had dared:

Hail Jaffa – King Of The Juice

It's What It's Not That Makes It What It Is

Un Oeuf Is As Good As A Feast

Tampax ... Insofar As (in response to the tampon ad that said **Modess ... Because**)

People Are Sticking To Kleenex

Her Cup Runneth Over (suggested by Shirley Polykoff to a corset manufacturer – 'it took an hour to unsell him')

From Those Wonderful Folks Who Gave You Pearl Harbor (a suggestion for Panasonic by Jerry Della Femina and used as the title of a book by him)

And one of Jimmy Carter's aides, keen that the President should utter as illustrious a phrase as John F. Kennedy's **Ich Bin Ein Berliner** on a visit to West Germany, suggested he go to Frankfurt and say ...

ENEMY EARS ARE LISTENING

Slogans rained down upon the hapless British as profusely as German bombs during the Second World War. The Ministry of Information, in blunderbuss fashion, fired away with as much material as possible in the hope of hitting something. Some of the slogans were brilliant, others were quite the reverse, and some unofficial phrases joined the propaganda war:

A Bayonet Is A Weapon With A Worker At Each End   Pacifist slogan, 1940.

Be Like Dad, Keep Mum and **Keep Mum, She's Not So Dumb**   (illustrated by an elegant un-Mum-like blonde being ogled by representatives of the three services) emanated from the Ministry of Information, c. 1941. The security theme was paramount in UK and US wartime propaganda. Civilians as well as military personnel were urged not to talk about war-related matters lest the enemy somehow got to hear.

Britain Can Take It   'While the public appreciated due recognition of their resolute qualities, they resented too great an emphasis on the stereotyped image of the Britisher in adversity as a wise-cracking Cockney. They were irritated by propaganda which represented their grim experience as a sort of particularly torrid Rugby match.' Hence the Ministry's abandonment of the slogan 'Britain Can Take It' in December 1940. (McLaine)

Careless Talk Costs Lives   Introduced in mid-1940, this became the most enduring of the security slogans, especially when accompanied by Fougasse cartoons – showing two men in a club, for example, one saying to the other '. . . strictly between four walls' (behind them is a painting through which Hitler's head is peeping), or two women gossiping in front of Hitler wallpaper.

Coughs And Sneezes Spread Diseases   A Ministry of Health warning from c. 1942, coupled with the line 'Trap The Germs In Your Handkerchief'.

Dig For Victory   Shortage of foodstuffs was an immediate concern upon the outbreak of war. On 4 October 1939, the Minister of Agriculture, Sir Reginald Dorman Smith, broadcast: 'Half a million more allotments properly worked will provide potatoes and vegetables that will feed another million adults and one and a half million children for eight months out of twelve . . . So, let's get going. Let "Dig For Victory" be the motto of everyone with a garden and of every able-bodied man and woman capable of digging an allotment in their spare time.' As a result, the number of allotments rose from 815,000 in 1939 to 1,400,000 in 1943.

DIG FOR VICTORY

Freedom Is In Peril – Defend It With All Your Might
(1939) Selected by George Orwell at the end of the war as an
example of a 'futile slogan obviously incapable of stirring strong
feelings or being circulated by word of mouth ... One has to take
into account the fact that nearly all English people dislike anything
that sounds high-flown or boastful. Slogans like **They Shall Not
Pass**, or **Better To Die On Your Feet Than Live On Your Knees**,
which have thrilled continental nations, seem slightly embarras-
sing to an Englishman, especially a working man.' To which Angus
Calder adds: 'It was partly from the de-sensitized prose of most of
the British press during the war, from the desertion of subtleties of

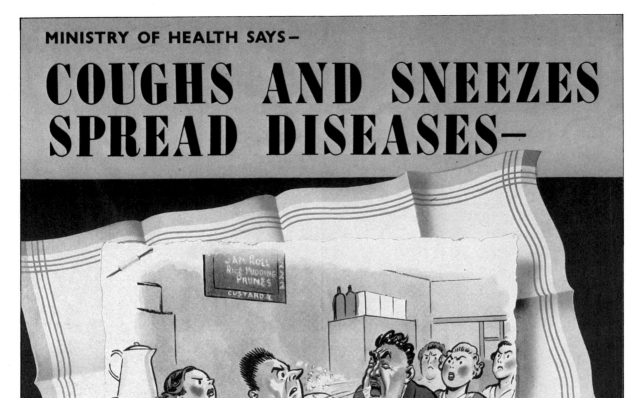

meaning in favour of slogans, that George Orwell derived the notion of Newspeak, the vocabulary of totalitarianism' in *Nineteen Eighty-Four*.

Go To It   In the summer of 1940, the Minister of Supply, Herbert Morrison, called for a voluntary labour force in words that echoed the public mood after Dunkirk. The quotation was used in a campaign run by the S. H. Benson agency (which later indulged in self-parody on behalf of Bovril with **Glow To It** in 1951–2).

Intern The Lot Anti-alien slogan, 1940.

Is Your Journey Really Necessary? First coined in 1939 to discourage evacuated Civil Servants from going home for Christmas. 'From 1941, the question was constantly addressed to all civilians, for, after considering a scheme for rationing on the ''points'' principle, or to ban all travel without a permit over more than fifty miles, the government had finally decided to rely on voluntary appeals, and on making travel uncomfortable by reducing the number of trains.' (Longmate)

Keep 'Em Flying Slogan in support of the US Air Force.

Keep It Dark was a phrase which appeared in more than one formulation, also in verse:

> If you've news of our munitions
> > KEEP IT DARK
> Ships or planes or troop positions
> > KEEP IT DARK
> Lives are lost through conversation
> Here's a tip for the duration
> When you've private information
> > KEEP IT DARK.

'Let Us Go Forward Together' A direct quotation from Churchill's first speech on becoming Prime Minister (May 1940), presented as such, and used to accompany his picture, in bulldog pose.

Make Do And Mend A phrase which set the tone for British life during the Second World War and after. Based on the Royal Navy expression for an afternoon free of work and still often used for mending clothes.

Second Front Now The demand chalked on walls (and supported by the Beaverbrook press) during 1942–3 for an invasion of the European mainland, particularly one in collaboration with the Soviet Union. The Allied military command disagreed and preferred to drive Axis troops out of North Africa and the Mediterranean first. Churchill's argument against a second front was that Britain's resources were fully stretched already.

Walls Have Ears was the neatest encapsulation of the security theme (the idea goes back as far as 1727, when Jonathan Swift wrote 'Walls have tongues, and hedges ears'). Also, **Tittle Tattle Lost The Battle** and **Keep It Under Your Hat** (US: **Keep It Under Your Stetson**). **Loose Talk Costs Lives** and **Idle Gossip Sinks Ships** were additional US versions of the same theme, together with **The Slip**

Of A Lip May Sink A Ship and **Enemy Ears Are Listening**. The only drawback to these generally clever slogans was that they tended to reinforce the notion that there *were* spies and fifth columnists under every bed even if there were not.

Your Courage, Your Cheerfulness, Your Resolution Will Bring Us Victory   One of the first posters after the outbreak of war, printed in vivid red and white. It caused a bitter outcry from those who resented any implication of 'Them and Us'. The slogan was suggested by A. P. Waterfield, a career Civil Servant at the Ministry of Information. He wanted 'A rallying war-cry that will . . . put us in an offensive mood at once.' *The Times* thundered: 'The insipid and patronising invocations to which the passer-by is now being treated have a power of exasperation which is all their own. There may be no intrinsic harm in their faint, academic piety, but the implication that the public morale needs this kind of support, or, if it did, that this is the kind of support it would need, is calculated to promote a response which is neither academic nor pious.'

BURN YOUR BRA

If a slogan is judged purely by its effectiveness, **Votes For Women** is a very good slogan. The words may not sparkle, but they achieved their end.

Both Emmeline and Christabel Pankhurst, founders of the Women's Social and Political Union, have described how this particular battle-cry emerged. In October 1905, a large meeting at the Free Trade Hall, Manchester, was due to be addressed by Sir Edward Grey, who was likely to attain ministerial office if the Liberals won the forthcoming general election. The WSPU was thus keen to challenge him in public on his party's attitude to women's suffrage in Britain.

'Good seats were secured for the Free Trade Hall meeting. The question was painted on a banner in large letters, in case it should not be made clear enough by vocal utterance. How should we word it? "Will you give women suffrage?" – we rejected that form, for the word "suffrage" suggested to some unlettered or jesting folk the idea of suffering. "Let them suffer away!" – we had heard the taunt. We must find another wording and we did! It was so obvious and yet, strange to say, quite new. Our banners bore this terse device: "WILL YOU GIVE VOTES FOR WOMEN?"' The plan had been to let down a banner from the gallery as soon as Sir Edward Grey stood up to speak. Unfortunately, the WSPU failed to obtain the requisite tickets. It had to abandon the large banner and cut out the three words which would fit on a small placard. 'Thus quite accidentally came into existence the slogan of the suffrage movement around the world.'

Alas, Sir Edward Grey did not answer the question, and it took rather more than this slogan – hunger-strikes, suicide, the First World War – before women got the vote in 1918. Other slogans employed were **Deeds, Not Words**; **Arise! Go Forth And Conquer**; and **The Bill, The Whole Bill, And Nothing But The Bill**. (At a meeting in the Royal Albert Hall, someone boomed 'Votes For Women' down an organ pipe.)

In the US, the Nineteenth Amendment, extending female franchise on a national scale, was ratified in time for the 1920 elections.

The modern Women's Liberation movement, advocating the rights and equality of women and commitment to an alteration in

woman's role in society, has given rise, in the US and the UK, to the following slogans, all since c. 1970:

Burn Your Bra   By analogy with burning a draft-card as a protest against the Vietnam War.

Equal Pay for Equal Work   Echoing a cry of teachers' organisations in the late nineteenth century.

This Ad Insults Women

A Woman's Right To Choose   (US, National Abortion Campaign)

Women Reclaim The Night (or, US, **Take Back The Night**)   From the campaign to make it possible for women to go out in the dark without fear of attack or rape.

COMING TO THIS CINEMA SHORTLY

The promotion of films takes slogan writing into realms of hyperbole seldom encountered in the marketing of political creeds or even consumer goods. The art of the come-on is at its peak in the tags applied to horror movies:

If This One Doesn't Scare You, You're Already Dead   *Phantasm 1*

Thank God It's Only A Movie. Please Let It Stay A Movie!   *Fleish*

It Takes All Kinds Of Critters To Make Farmer Vincent Fritters   *Motel Hell*

Paraquat! ... Agent Orange! ... But Nothing Prepared The World For This!   *Forest of Fear*

£10,000 If You Die Of Fright!   *Macabre*

Can You Survive *The Texas Chain Saw Massacre* ... It Happened!

They Were Going To Rape Her One By One. She Was Going To Kill Them ... One By One.   *Death Weekend*

It Crawls! It Creeps! It Eats You Alive! Run – Don't Walk From *The Blob*.

Where Your Nightmare Ends *Willard* Begins.

***The Curse Of Frankenstein* Will Haunt You Forever (Please Try Not To Faint).**

The most notorious of all film campaigns is the one for the Howard Hughes production of *The Outlaw* in 1943. As if **The Two Great Reasons For Jane Russell's Rise To Stardom** (skilfully supported by the Hughes-designed cantilever bra) were not enough in the various pictures of the skimpily clad new star (one version had her reclining with a long whip), the producer attached a smouldering succession of slogans:

Tall ... Terrific ... And Trouble!

Who Wouldn't Fight For A Woman Like This?

Mean! Moody! Magnificent!

The Girl With The Summer-Hot Lips ... And The Winter-Cold Heart

How'd You Like To Tussle With Russell?

Although it is hard to believe, *Julius Caesar* was promoted as **Greater Than** *Ivanhoe* and *Joseph Andrews* got away with **The Epic Love Story In Which Everybody Has A Great Role And A Big Part**. I do know, however, that 'The Book They Said Could Never Be Written Has Become The Movie They Said Could Never Be Filmed' is pure invention that has not appeared on a poster – yet. See how many of the following slogans you can connect with the films they actually advertised. The answers are on page 36.

1 The Greatest Motion Picture Ever Made
2 They're Young ... They're In Love ... And They Kill People
3 A Thousand Thrills ... And Hayley Mills
4 A Lion In Your Lap
5 Like The Act Of Love, This Film Must Be Experienced From Beginning To End
6 Love Means Never Having To Say You're Sorry
7 Love Means Not Having To Say You're Ugly
8 Getting There Is Half the Fun ... ********** Is All Of It
9 ********** is *Not* A Musical
10 A Completely New Experience Between Men And Women!
11 We Are Not Alone
12 Garbo Talks!
13 Garbo Laughs!
14 God Created Woman – But The Devil Created Brigitte Bardot
15 Gable's Back And Garson's Got Him
16 A Cast Of 125,000
17 If There Were An 11th Commandment, They Would Have Broken That, Too
18 Don't Give Away The Ending. It's The Only One We Have
19 He Treated Her Rough – And She Loved It!
20 When The Hands Point Straight Up ... The Excitement Starts At **********
21 What We've Got Here Is A Failure To Communicate
22 Pray For **********
23 In Space No One Can Hear You Scream
24 Don't Pronounce It – See It!
25 Boy. Do We Need It Now
26 They Had A Date With Fate In ... **********
27 You'll Believe A Man Can Fly
28 Every Father's Daughter Is A Virgin
29 The Thousands Who Have Read The Book Will Know Why We Will Not Sell Any Children Tickets To See This Picture!
30 ********** Is Coming
31 The Story Of A Homosexual Who Married A Nymphomaniac
32 The Motion Picture With Something To Offend Everyone

ANSWERS

1 *Gone with the Wind*
2 *Bonnie and Clyde*
3 *In Search of the Castaways*
4 *Bwana Devil* (first 3-D film)
5 *The Sailor who Fell from Grace with the Sea*
6 *Love Story*
7 *The Abominable Dr Phibes*
8 *Being There*
9 *The Boys in the Band*
10 *The Men* (about paraplegics)
11 *Close Encounters of the Third Kind*
12 *Anna Christie*
13 *Ninotchka*
14 *And God Created Woman*
15 *Adventure*
16 *Ben Hur* (1927 version – origin of the phrase 'Cast of Thousands?')
17 *The Postman Always Rings Twice* (1981 version)
18 *Psycho*
19 *Red Dust*
20 *High Noon*
21 *Cool Hand Luke*
22 *Rosemary's Baby*
23 *Alien*
24 *Phffft!/Ninotchka*
25 *That's Entertainment*
26 *Casablanca*
27 *Superman – The Movie*
28 *Goodbye Columbus*
29 *The Grapes of Wrath*
30 *The Birds*
31 *The Music Lovers* (about Tchaikovsky)
32 *The Loved One*

THE CUSTOMER IS ALWAYS RIGHT

H. Gordon Selfridge (1856–1947) was an American who after a spell with Marshall Field & Co. in Chicago came to Britain and introduced the idea of the monster department store. It was he who said **The Customer Is Always Right** and many another phrases now generally associated with the business of selling through stores. He may have invented the notion of so many **Shopping Days To Christmas** – at least, when he was still in Chicago he sent out an instruction to Marshall Field's heads of departments and assistants: 'The Christmas season has begun and but twenty-three more shopping days remain in which to make our holiday sales record.' The store which he opened in Oxford Street, London, in 1909 gave rise to the slogans **This Famous Store Needs No Name On The Door** (because it had none) and **Complete Satisfaction Or Money Cheerfully Refunded**.

Other shopping slogans in stores . . . and in the home:

Avon Calling!   was first heard in the US in 1886. The first Avon Lady, Mrs P. F. A. Allre, was employed by the firm's founder, D. H. McConnell, to visit and sell cosmetics in the home. (Flexner)

Don't Ask The Price It's A Penny   That great British institution, Marks & Spencer, had its origins in a stall set up in Leeds market in 1884 by a 21-year-old Jewish refugee from Poland, Michael Marks. His slogan has become part of commercial folklore. It was written on a sign over the penny section – not all his goods were that cheap. He simply hit upon the idea of classifying goods according to price.

It's Just A Part Of The Austin Reed Service   became a catchphrase from its inception in 1930 and was devised by Donald McCullough, the firm's advertising manager (who subsequently found fame as the question-master in the popular BBC radio series, *The Brains Trust*). It was still in use on behalf of the London store in 1950.

Never Knowingly Undersold   was formulated by the founder of the John Lewis Partnership, John Spedan Lewis, in about 1920 to express a pricing policy which originated with his father, John Lewis, who first opened a small shop in London's Oxford Street in

fitting below the belt

Some gentlemen are very much more efficiently streamlined than others.

That is why we make dress waistcoats in ten different styles, in many cases with a choice of three depths of front.

Incidentally we can fit all sizes of chest up to 48″ with the utmost precision.

*It's just a part of the
Austin Reed
service*

103-113 REGENT STREET · LONDON · W.1
Telephone : Regent 6189
Glasgow Birmingham Liverpool Manchester Sheffield Leeds Bristol Belfast

1864. The slogan is believed to have been used within the firm before it was given public expression in the 1930s: 'If you can buy more cheaply elsewhere anything you have just bought from us we will refund the difference.' The firm does not regard 'Never Knowingly Undersold' as an advertising device in the generally accepted sense of the word, although it is displayed on the sides of its vehicles and, together with the undertaking set out above, printed on the backs of sales bills. Its main purpose is 'as a discipline upon the Partnership's Central Buyers to insure that the best possible value is offered to customers'. The firm does not advertise its merchandise. Hence, the phrase has an almost mystical significance for the Partnership.

Nothing Over Sixpence   The first British Woolworth's opened in 1909 and was described as a 'threepence and sixpence' store, the equivalent of the 'five-and-ten' (cent) stores in the US. Hence the phrase 'Nothing Over Sixpence' arose and endured until the Second World War, when prices could no longer be contained below this limit. A song dating from 1927 includes the lines:

> To Woolworth's, Hobbs and Sutcliffe always go to get their bats,
> Stan Baldwin gets his pipes there, and Winston gets his hats;
> And the Prince would never think of going elsewhere for his
>   spats —
> And there's nothing over sixpence in the stores!

Pile It High, Sell It Cheap   Sir John Cohen (1898–1979), founder of Tesco Supermarkets, built his fortune upon this golden rule. In 1963 Tesco was one of the biggest traders to proclaim **We Give Green Shield Stamps**.

The Universal Provider   Whiteley's, first in Westbourne Grove and later in Queensway, introduced department store shopping to London, in 1863. William Whiteley (1831–1907), the self-styled 'Universal Provider', claimed to supply anything from **A Pin To An Elephant**. One morning, as Whiteley described it: 'An eminent pillar of the Church called upon me and said, "Mr Whiteley, I want an elephant." "Certainly, sir. When would you like it?" "Oh, today!" "And where?" "I should like it placed in my stable." "It shall be done!" In four hours a tuskiana was placed in the reverend gentleman's coach-house. Of course, this was a try-on designed to test our resources, and it originated in a bet. The Vicar confessed himself greatly disconcerted because, as he frankly avowed, he did not think we would execute the order. He displayed the utmost anxiety lest I should hold him to the transaction. But I let him down with a small charge for pilotage and food only, at which he confessed himself deeply grateful.'

The World's Largest Store   Macy's, New York City. Current 1981.

YES! WE HAVE NO BANANAS!

Britain became 'banana-conscious' in the early years of the twentieth century following the appointment of Roger Ackerley as chief salesman of Elders & Fyffes, banana importers, in 1898. The phrase **Have A Banana**, never a slogan as such, was popularly interpolated at the end of the first line of the song 'Let's All Go Down The Strand', published in 1904. It had not been put there by the composer but was so successful that later printings of the song always included it. Every time it was sung the phrase reinforced the sales campaign, free of charge.

Other banana songs followed. In 1922, a further Elders & Fyffes campaign benefited from the composition 'Yes, We Have No Bananas' (a remark the composer claimed to have heard from the lips of a Greek fruit-seller). Fyffes cooperated with the music publishers and distributed 10,000 'hands' of bananas to music-sellers with the inscription **Yes! We Have No Bananas! On Sale Here**.

The title of the next song, 'I've Never Seen A Straight Banana' – like the line 'I had a banana/With Lady Diana' from the earlier 'Burlington Bertie from Bow' – underlined the sexual suggestiveness of the product, which no doubt explains some of its popular appeal or at least the humour surrounding it. **Unzipp A Banana** – also, **Unzipp Ya Banana** – went the whole hog; in 1959, Mather & Crowther launched it in a joint promotion on behalf of the three main UK banana importers.

EVERY HOME SHOULD HAVE ONE

Chases Dirt   Old Dutch Cleanser; US, from 1905. The ad showed a Dutch woman with a stick, literally chasing dirt away.

Cleans Round The Bend   Harpic lavatory cleaner; UK, from 1930s. Gave rise to the expression 'round the bend' meaning 'mad', popular from the Second World War on.

Hasn't Scratched Yet   Bon Ami cleanser; US, from c. 1890, still current 1941.

Hold It Up To The Light, Not A Stain And Shining Bright   Surf washing powder; UK, current late 1950s. A line from the 'Mrs Bradshaw' series of TV ads in which the eponymous lady never appeared but her male lodger did. (From the radio *Goon Show* of the same period: 'The BBC – hold it up to the light – not a brain in sight!')

It Beats As It Sweeps As It Cleans   Hoover carpet sweepers; US, from 1919, still current 1981. Coined by Gerald Page-Wood of Erwin Wasey in Cleveland, Ohio. 'The Hoover' started as an invention by James Murray Spangler in 1908. It was taken up by William H. Hoover whose company, until that time, manufactured high-grade leather goods, harnesses and horse collars. Spangler's idea was developed to include the principle of carpet vibration to remove dust. This gave 'Hoovers' their exclusive feature – the gentle beating or tapping of the carpet to loosen dirt and grit embedded in it. An agitator bar performed this function, together with strong suction and revolving brushes – giving the Hoover the 'triple action' enshrined in the slogan.

Kills All Known Germs   Domestos household bleach; UK, from 1959.

Omo Adds Brightness To Whiteness   Omo washing powder; UK, current late 1950s.

$6.25 is all you need pay down to secure a Hoover complete with household cleaning attachments. Now, anyone can afford a Hoover Have yours delivered today!

It beats rugs gently; sweeps as no broom can; and thoroughly air-cleans – *electrically!* Its handy new air-cleaning tools dust, *dustlessly.* It keeps your home immaculate; saves time, strength, health; makes rugs wear years *longer.* Certainly, it's a Hoover! Delivered to any home upon payment of only $6.25 down! Your Authorized Hoover Dealer will explain **our easy purchase plan.**

THE HOOVER COMPANY, NORTH CANTON, OHIO
The oldest and largest maker of electric cleaners
The Hoover is also made in Canada, at Hamilton, Ontario

Poor Cold Fred Electricity Council storage heaters; UK, from 1969. A memorable but briefly exposed line from copy written at Hobson Bates by Roger Musgrave. A TV campaign showed 'Fred', who thought that storage heaters would cost hundreds of pounds and thus remained cold until enlightened about them. Musgrave admits he was probably influenced by memories of the old rhyme 'Here lies Fred/Who was alive and is dead'.

See That Hump? The Long Patented Hook & Eye Company; US, from 1891.

Softness Is A Thing Called Comfort Comfort fabric conditioner; UK, current 1981.

Someone's Mother Persil washing powder; UK, current 1940 – a theme carried from posters and press ads on to TV:

> What someone's mum really ought to know,
> So someone's mum better get to know,
> That Persil washes whiter, whiter –
> Persil washes whiter.

Also the phrase **What Is A Mum?** featured in a series of TV ads from 1961.

Stronger Than Dirt Ajax cleanser; US, quoted 1979.

This Is Luxury You Can Afford By Cyril Lord Cyril Lord carpets; UK, current early 1960s.

Tide's In, Dirt's Out Tide washing powder; UK, current 1950s. Also 'Get your clothes clean. Not only clean but **Deep Down Clean**, Tide clean.'

Use Sapolio Sapolio soap; US, quoted in 1952 as 'once ubiquitous in the USA'. The words **Spotless Town** were also synonymous with Sapolio. They came from rhymes devised by J. K. Fraser, like this one:

> This is the maid of fair renown
> Who scrubs the floors of Spotless Town
> To find a speck when she is through
> Would take a pair of specs or two,
> And her employment isn't slow.
> For she employs SAPOLIO.

'"Spotless Town" (while selling Sapolio by the ton) was parodied in many papers and a syndicated political series ran all over the country. At one time four theatrical companies booked shows called *Spotless Town* ... and one community changed its name permanently thereto.' (Watkins)

This is the maid of fair renown
Who scrubs the floors of Spotless Town.
To find a speck when she is through
Would take a pair of specs or two,
And her employment isn't slow.
For she employs

SAPOLIO

Very **********, Very Sanderson Sanderson furnishing fabrics and wall-coverings; UK, current, 1975. Various celebrities were photographed amid what purported to be their natural surroundings. Among them: Joan Bakewell, Petula Clark, Jilly Cooper, Britt Ekland and Kingsley Amis. I happened to be visiting Mr Amis in his home the day after the first advertisement featuring him had appeared in the colour magazines. I took the opportunity to exclaim 'Very Kingsley Amis, Very Sanderson' as we stepped into his sitting-room. The novelist seemed perturbed at my reaction and was at pains to point out that, although he and the other celebrities had had a room decorated by Sanderson in addition to their fees, the photograph in the ad bore little resemblance to the conditions under which he actually lived (I saw that it did not). He described the wallpaper chosen to reflect his refined tastes as 'superior Indian restaurant'. Alan Coren, writing in *Punch*, warned Alexander Solzhenitsyn, at that time just arrived in the West, that he might find the role of the writer a bit different this side of the Iron Curtain. He would know that he had finally settled in when he heard people declaring 'Very Solzhenitsyn, Very Sanderson'.

The Watch Of Railroad Accuracy Used in watch advertisements by the Hamilton Watch Co.; US, from 1908. The phrase first arose from a testimonial sent to the company by a railroad worker.

The Watch That Made The Dollar Famous Ingersoll dollar watches; US, from *c.* 1892. Soon after the first dollar watch appeared, Mr R. H. Ingersoll was being introduced at some ceremony by a flushed hostess who forgot his name. So she said: 'Oh, the man that made the dollar famous.' Next day, Mr Ingersoll presented the company with its long-lasting slogan.

THE EYES AND EARS OF THE WORLD

The world of leisure pursuits and communications – records, radio and TV, photography and going to the pictures ...

Ars Gratia Artis Metro-Goldwyn-Mayer film company; US, from *c.* 1916. Howard Dietz, director of publicity and advertising with the original Goldwyn Pictures company, had left Columbia University not long before. When asked to design a trademark, he based it on the university's lion and added the Latin words meaning 'Art for Art's Sake' underneath. The trademark and motto were carried over when Samuel Goldwyn retired to make way for the merger of Metropolitan with the interests of Louis B. Mayer. 'Goldwyn Pictures Griddle The Earth' is the probably apocryphal but typical suggestion said to have come from Samuel Goldwyn for a slogan.

Brings The World To The World Gaumont-British cinema newsreel; UK, from the 1930s.

Don't Write – Telegraph Western Union Telegraph Co.; US, from 1920 – though the words first appeared unofficially written up on office windows of various branches in 1917–19.

The Eyes And Ears Of The World Paramount News cinema newsreel; UK, from 1927 to 1957.

The Greatest Show On Earth Name given by P. T. Barnum (1810–91) to the circus formed by the merger with his rival, Bailey's; US, from 1881. Still the slogan of what is now Ringling Bros and Barnum & Bailey Circus. Used as the title of a Cecil B. De Mille circus movie, 1952.

His Master's Voice One of the best-known trademarks and brand names of the twentieth century. The words have something of the force of a slogan. In 1899, the English painter Francis Barraud approached the Gramophone Company in London to borrow one of their machines so that he could paint his dog, Nipper, listening to it. Nipper was accustomed, in fact, to a *phonograph* but his master thought that the larger horn of the gramophone would make a better picture. Subsequently, the Gramophone Company bought the painting and adapted it as a trademark. In 1901, the Victor Talking Machine Company (slogan **Loud Enough For Dancing**) acquired the American rights. The company later became RCA Victor and took Nipper with them. Nowadays, Britain's EMI owns the trademark in most countries, RCA owns it in North and South America, and JVC owns it in Japan.

The Instrument Of The Immortals Steinway pianos; US, from 1919. The slogan was coined 'in a flash' by Raymond Rubicam at N. W. Ayer & Son: 'I learned that the piano had been used by practically all the greatest pianists and most of the great composers since Wagner ... without effort, the phrase formed in my mind ... when the ad was finished I showed it to Jerry Lauck, the account executive, and by that time I was so enthusiastic about the idea that I urged him to persuade Steinway to use the phrase not just for one but for a whole series ... Lauck shared my enthusiasm for the idea, but said that Steinway did not believe in ''slogans''. I remember saying ''all right, don't call it a slogan, call it an advertising phrase.'' ' (Watkins)

It's The Lubitsch Touch That Means So Much   Used on posters for films directed by Ernst Lubitsch; US, from *c.* 1925.

Let Your Fingers Do The Walking   Yellow Pages (classified telephone directories) from American Telephone & Telegraph Co.; US, current 1960s. Also **Want To Reach 8 Out Of 10 Adults? – Walk This Way**. (UK graffito, quoted 1981: '8 out of 10 buying executives walk this way', to which was added: 'They should loosen their belts.')

More Stars Than There Are In Heaven   MGM studio motto; US, current 1930s. Devised by Howard Dietz.

Say It With Flowers   National Publicity Committee of the Society of American florists; US, from late 1920s. Henry Penn of Boston, Mass., originated the phrase as chairman of the committee. He was discussing the need for such a slogan with Major P. K. O'Keefe, head of an agency. The Major suggested: 'Flowers are words that even a babe can understand' – a line he had found in a poetry book. Mr Penn considered this too long. The Major, agreeing, rejoined: 'Why, you can say it with flowers in so many words.' Mr Penn's hand went bang! on the table. They had found their slogan. (Lambert)

They Come As A Boon And A Blessing To Men,/The Pickwick, The Owl, And The Waverley Pen   Macniven & Cameron Ltd's pens, manufactured in Edinburgh and Birmingham; UK, current *c.* 1920. Also **Macniven & Cameron's Pens Are Recommended By 3,050 Newspapers**.

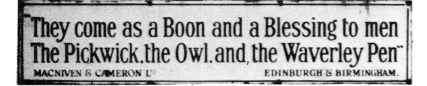

They Laughed When I Sat Down At The Piano, But When I Started To Play!   US School of Music piano tutor; US, from 1925. A classic advertising headline written by John Caples at Ruthrauff & Ryan. The copy underneath includes the following: 'As the last notes of

They Laughed When I Sat Down At the Piano But When I Started to Play!–

ARTHUR had just played "The Rosary." The room rang with applause. I decided that this would be a dramatic moment for me to make my debut. To the amazement of all my friends, I strode confidently over to the piano and sat down

"Jack is up to his old tricks," somebody chuckled. The crowd ....

A Complete Triumph!

As the last notes of the Moonlight Sonata died away, the room resounded with a sudden roar of applause. I found myself surrounded by excited fa.... How my friends carried on! Men sh.... ly congrat...ted me ....

musician himself were speaking to me—speaking through the medium of music—not in words but in chords. Not in sentences but in exquisite melodies!

the lessons continued they got easier and easier. Before I knew it I was playing all the pieces I liked best. Nothing stopped me. I could play ballads or classical numbers or jazz, all with equal ease! And I never did have any special talent for music!

Play Any Instrument

You too, can n.. teach yourself to be an accom ...icia... home—in.. If the usual ...ple me

the Moonlight Sonata died away, the room resounded with a sudden roar of applause. I found myself surrounded by excited faces.... Men shook my hand – wildly congratulated me – pounded me on the back in their enthusiasm! Everybody was exclaiming with delight – plying me with rapid questions ... "Jack! Why didn't you tell us you could play like that?" ... "Where *did* you learn?" And then I explained how for years I had longed to play the piano. "A few months ago," I continued, "I saw an interesting ad for the US School of Music – a new method of learning to play which only costs a few cents a day!"' The ad gave rise to various jokes – 'They laughed when I sat down to play – somebody had taken away the stool' – and Caples also wrote a follow-up: 'They Grinned When The Waiter Spoke To Me In French – But Their Laughter Changed To Amazement At My Reply.'

The Weekend Starts Here Associated-Rediffusion TV pop show *Ready, Steady, Go*; UK, current 1964. Transmitted live early on Friday evenings.

We Never Closed Windmill Theatre, London; UK, from Second World War. Vivien Van Damm, the proprietor, coined this slogan for the venerable comedy and strip venue which was the only West End showplace to remain open during the blitz. An obvious variant: 'We Never Clothed.'

You Press The Button – We Do The Rest Kodak cameras; US, current 1890. 'It was literally edited out of a long piece of copy by George Eastman himself – one of the greatest of advertising ideas.' (Watkins)

BUILD UP YOUR EGO, AMIGO

Build Up Your Ego, Amigo   Adler Elevated Shoes; US, current 1940s. Coined by Shirley Polykoff.

Children's Shoes Have Far To Go   Start-Rite children's shoes; UK, current 1946. The idea of the boy and girl 'twins' walking up the middle of a road between rows of beech trees came to the company's advertising agent as he drove back to London from a meeting at Start-Rite's Norwich offices. He was reminded of the illustration in Kipling's *Just So Stories* of 'the cat who walked by himself' and developed the idea from there – despite many subsequent suggestions from the public that walking down the middle of the road would not enable children, or their shoes, to go very far.

I Dreamed I ********** In My Maidenform Bra   Maidenform bras; US, from 1949. A classic ad from the days when bras were not for burning but for dreaming about – if, that is, women had ever fantasised about being out in their underwear. Evidently, many had and the series, devised by Norman Craig & Kummel, ran for twenty years. Maidenform offered prizes up to $10,000 for dream situations they could utilise in the advertising, in addition to: 'I Dreamed I Took The Bull By The Horns/Went Walking/Stopped The Traffic/Went To Blazes/Was A Social Butterfly/Rode In A Gondola/Was Cleopatra . . . In My Maidenform Bra.'

If You Want To Get Ahead, Get A Hat   The Hat Council; UK, quoted 1965.

Looks Even Better On A Man   Tootal shirts; UK, from 1961. A girl was featured wearing an oversize man's shirt.

The Man In The Hathaway Shirt   C. F. Hathaway shirts; US, from 1950. It was the eye-patch on the male model that made David Ogilvy's campaign famous, but people always refer to 'The Man in the Hathaway shirt' as such and the reason is plain – this was the bold headline to the advertisement.

The man in the Hathaway shirt

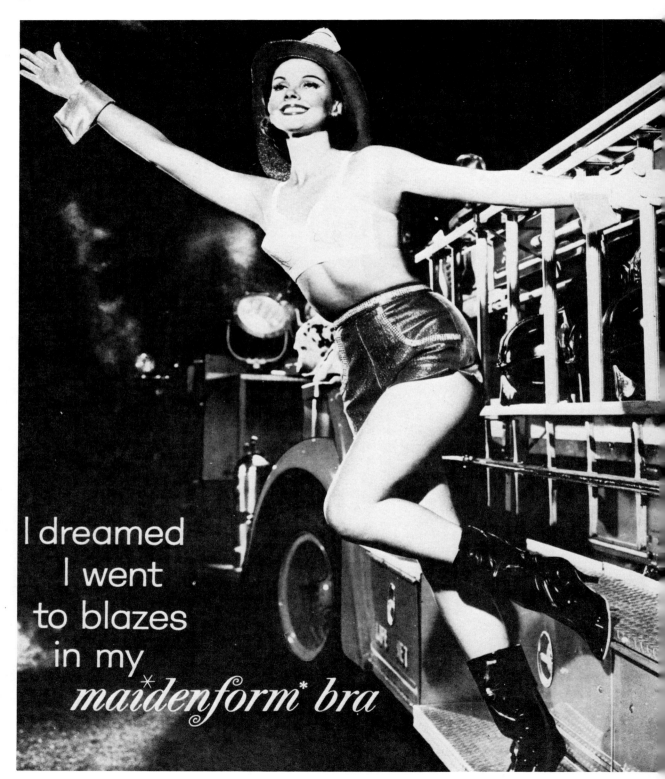

I dreamed
I went
to blazes
in my
maidenform bra

My Bottoms Are Tops   Gloria Vanderbilt jeans by Murjani; US, current 1980.

Next To Myself I Like BVD's Best   BVD's (comfortable, loose-fitting underwear); US, from *c.* 1920.

Quality Never Goes Out Of Style   Levi jeans; US, current 1980.

Rael-Brook Toplin, The Shirt You Don't Iron   Rael-Brook shirts; UK, current mid-1960s. That rarity – a slogan created by the manufacturer. Johnny Johnson, who wrote the music for the jingle used in the TV ad, says: 'Harry Rael-Brook would not work through an agency. He came into my office and said, "I want a 30-second jingle." I said, "Oh yes, and what do you want to say?" And he said, "Rael-Brook Toplin, the shirt you don't iron."' And that was that. The jingle consists of this phrase repeated over and over.

Step Out With A Stetson   Hats manufactured by John B. Stetson Co.; US, current 1930s.

Triumph Has The Bra For The Way You Are   Triumph foundation garments, swimwear and lingerie; UK, from *c.* 1977.

Walk The Barratt Way   Barratt shoes; UK, current early 1940s.

What Becomes A Legend Most?   Blackglama mink; US, current 1976. Headline from a series of press ads showing mink coats being worn by 'legendary' figures including Margot Fonteyn, Martha Graham, Rudolph Nureyev (all three in one ad), Shirley Maclaine and Ethel Merman.

GO NOW, PAY LATER

Better Yet Connecticut   From the *New York Times*, 22 April 1981: 'Connecticut came forth today with its official slogan ... It was created by Joseph Roy, a 45-year-old graphic artist ... "We had thought of 'I Love New York, But Better Yet Connecticut,' but it was too long," said Richard Combs, chairman of the Governor's Vacation Travel Council as he announced at a news conference that Mr Roy's slogan was "the winner of a blockbuster contest."'

'John J. Carson said the slogan would adorn T-shirts and be displayed in banks and on billboards and bumper stickers. Both state officials and Vacation Travel Council members voiced confidence that their slogan could vie in the marketplace with such tourism precursors as **I Love New York**, **Make It In Massachussetts** and **Virginia Is For Lovers**.

'Asked to describe the creative process that went into formation of the phrase, Mr Roy replied: "I went to bed thinking about it and when I woke in the morning I had it." The runner-up was "Connecticut Is a Whale of a State."'

I Love New York   New York State Department of Commerce; US, from 1977. Created by Charlie Moss of Wells, Rich, Greene. The campaign began in June 1977 with a commercial which showed various people enjoying themselves in outdoor activities – fishing, horseback riding, camping, and so forth. Each one said something like: 'I'm from New Hampshire, but I love New York,' 'I'm from Cape Cod, but I love New York,' and ended with a funny little man, shown in a camping scene, saying: 'I'm from Brooklyn, but I *looooove* New York.' Since when it has become one of the best known advertising slogans in the world.

Jane Maas, who supervised the campaign from its inception, points out: 'In New York State, 91 per cent of the people are aware of the phrase – that's more people than know Christopher Columbus discovered America. "ILNY" is on T-shirts in literally every country of the world. We hear that the "ILNY" bumper sticker was seen on the Great Wall of China. The Japanese version of our song is the number two on their Hit Parade.'

As familiar in its abbreviated forms, most often with 'love' replaced by a heart-shape, 'I Love New York' has also been widely copied (as has the use of the heart-shape for 'love'). There is 'I Love Osaka', 'J'aime Paris', and in the US the phrase has been picked up by hundreds of places and products, ranging from hotels to hot dogs.

Inter-City Makes The Going Easy, And The Coming Back   British Rail; UK, from 1972 (London and South-East Region) and 1975 (Inter-City).

It's So Bracing Skegness (seaside resort in Lincolnshire, promoted along with London & North Eastern Railway company); UK,
current 1909. The slogan is inseparable from the accompanying
jolly fisherman drawn by John Hassall (1868–1948). Actually, he
did not visit Skegness until twenty-eight years after he did the
poster. His first visit was when he was made a freeman of the town.

Let The Train Take The Strain British Rail Awayday fares; UK,
1970.

The Road Of Anthracite The Delaware Lackawanna & Western
railroad; US, from 1900. The character of 'Phoebe Snow' was
created to promote the idea of cleanliness in travelling on a railroad
which used sootless anthracite coal as locomotive fuel. She
appeared for half a century and the railroad came to call itself **The
Route Of Phoebe Snow**. Her adventures were described in short
verses, such as:

Yes, Phoebe, I
Can now see why
The praises of
This road you cry.
My gloves are white
As when last night
We took the Road
Of Anthracite.

(Watkins)

See America First Great Northern Railway Co.; US, from c. 1914.
Variously credited to G. Herb Palin, a leading US slogan writer, and
Louis W. Hill Senior, president of the company. The slogan was
splashed all over the US and helped turn the tide of travel from the
east coast to the west. Hill said he just picked up the phrase from an
ad and adopted it as his company's slogan. Perhaps Palin wrote the
original?

Sleep Like A Kitten Chesapeake & Ohio Lines; US, from 1933.
This slogan appeared with the logo of a kitten tucked up in bed. A
vice-president of the company came across a picture entitled 'The
Sleepy Cat' in a New York newspaper and asked around the office
what phrase best signified sound sleep. Among the suggestions
were 'like a top' and 'like a kitten'. The latter was voted the winner.

This Is The Age Of The Train British Rail; UK, from 1980.
Somewhat wishful thinking. The public countered with graffiti:
'Yes, it takes an age to catch one' and 'Ours was 104'.

THAT GOOD MORNING FEELING

The Best To You Each Morning   Kellogg's corn flakes and other brands; US, from 1953.

Breakfast Of Champions   Wheaties; US, current 1950. A series featuring sporting champions showed 'Jackie Robinson – one of the greatest names in baseball . . . this famous Dodger star is a Wheaties man: "A lot of us ball players go for milk, fruit and Wheaties," says Jackie . . . Had *your* Wheaties today?' Kurt Vonnegut used the phrase as the title of a novel, 1973.

Food Shot From Guns   Quaker Puffed Wheat and Puffed Rice; US, current 1920s onwards. Claude C. Hopkins: 'I watched the process where the grains were shot from guns. And I coined the phrase. The idea aroused ridicule. One of the greatest food advertizers in the country wrote an article about it. He said that of all the follies evolved in food advertizing this certainly was the worst – the idea of appealing to women on "Food Shot From Guns" was the theory of an imbecile. But the theory proved attractive. It was such a curiosity rouser that it proved itself the most successful campaign ever conducted in cereals.'

That 'Good-Morning' Feeling   Welgar Shredded Wheat; UK, current mid-1940s.

Snap! Crackle! Pop!   Kellogg's Rice Krispies; US, from *c.* 1928. A version early in the century went 'It Pops! It Snaps! It Crackles!'

Sunny Jim   Force breakfast cereal; US, from *c.* 1903. Few people who use the nickname 'Sunny Jim' know that it originated in ads for Force. The Force Food Company was formed in 1901. A London office was established the following year. By 1903, advertising on both sides of the Atlantic was featuring the character called 'Sunny Jim'. He was the invention of two young American girls, a Miss Ficken and Minnie Maud Hanff (usually credited with the phrase), who had submitted a jingle and rough sketch to the company. One of the first jingles was:

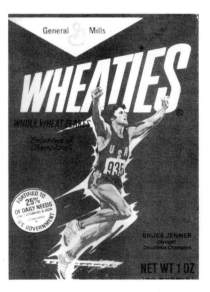

Vigor, Vim, Perfect Trim;
Force made him, Sunny Jim.

In the 1920s came:

High o'er the fence leaps Sunny Jim,
Force is the food that raises him.

In the 1930s Force was advertised on commercial radio broadcasts to the UK from Radios Luxembourg, Lyons and Normandy. In the US, the product has now disappeared from sale but in 1970 the A. C. Fincken Company relaunched it in the UK. When James Callaghan became Prime Minister in 1976 the phrase inevitably became much used (headline from *The Observer*, 18 March 1979: 'Sunny Jim tires of wheeler-dealing'). The name of the cereal was long a gift to jokesters:

A: I can't coax my husband to eat any breakfast.
B: Have you tried Force?
A: Madam, you don't know my husband.

Sunny Jim tires of wheeler-dealing

There's A Reason Postum and Post cereals; US, from 1899 to 1924. Charles William Post invented the beverage now known as Postum. This was a vague phrase he used as he explained the merits of the product when it was new. A 1908 ad for Postum Grape-Nuts uses it thus: 'One of Uncle Sam's Navy boys was given up by the doctor. His stomach would not retain food or medicine until a mess-mate suggested Grape-Nuts. On this world-famed food and milk he gained about 40 lb. in four months and got well. It requires no "Expert Chemist" to prove that "THERE'S A REASON" for Grape-Nuts.'

They're G-R-Reat! Kellogg's Sugar Frosted Flakes; US, from *c.* 1951.

THE GREAT NEW FRONTIER FAIR DEAL SOCIETY

For some US presidents it is not enough to attain the White House. They have to dignify their policies with a resounding label:

'We demand that big business give people a **Square Deal**,' said President Theodore Roosevelt, campaigning in 1901. 'If elected I shall see to it that every man has a Square Deal, no more and no less.'

Woodrow Wilson, campaigning successfully for the presidency in 1912, sought the **New Freedom**, safeguarding the democratic rights of small business against big business, 'a revival of the power of the people'.

'I pledge you, I pledge myself, to a **New Deal** for the American people,' Franklin D. Roosevelt said in a speech to the 1932 Democratic Convention which had just nominated him. The phrase became the keynote of the ensuing election campaign but it was not new – in Britain, Lloyd George had talked of 'A New Deal For Everyone' in 1919.

'Every segment of our population and every individual has a right to expect from this government a **Fair Deal**' – from President Truman's State of the Union message, 1949. Proposals included legislation on civil rights and fair employment practices.

Dwight Eisenhower called for a **Great Crusade** during his successful campaign in 1952.

'We stand today on the edge of a **New Frontier** – the frontier of the 1960s . . . [it] is not a set of challenges. It sums up not what I intend to offer the American people, but what I intend to ask them' – John F. Kennedy, accepting the Democratic nomination in 1960.

After tentatively trying out *his* phrase several times, President Lyndon B. Johnson elevated it to capital letters in a speech at the University of Michigan in May 1964 – 'In your time we have the opportunity to move not only towards the rich society and the powerful society but upward to the **Great Society**.'

In 1967, Governor George Romney put it all in a nutshell: 'There was the New Deal of Franklin Roosevelt, the Fair Deal of Harry Truman, and the ordeal of Lyndon Johnson.'

SQUARE DEAL FOR SLOGANS

HAIR CARE

Does She ... Or Doesn't She?/Only Her Hairdresser Knows For Sure Clairol; US, from 1955. 'This seemingly non-acceptable phrase turned a non-acceptable commodity into the highly respected industry that hair-coloring is today' – the claim of Shirley Polykoff, who coined it. Or did she? In her book entitled *Does She ... Or Doesn't She?*, Ms Polykoff wonders whether her mother-in-law didn't invent it twenty years before: 'I had just met George ... when he invited me to Passover dinner in Reading, Pa ... it was tantamount to a proposal of marriage ... I could hardly wait to start the drive home to find out how I had done ... "She (George's mother) says you paint your hair. Well, do you?" I merely scrunched down on my side of the car. I could hear his mother thinking as she cleared away the dishes: "Zee paint dos huer? Odder zee paint dos nicht?" Freely translated that means, "Does she ... or doesn't she?"'

When the Clairol account moved to Foote Cone & Belding in the mid-1950s, Shirley Polykoff was assigned to it and suffered the customary creative block that preceeds many a great coinage. As she tells it, she was at a party with George, now her husband, when in came a girl with flaming red hair and Shirley P. involuntarily uttered the line.

Next morning she wrote a memo to the head art director, giving two lines to be rejected and the one she wanted accepted to be followed by the phrase 'Only her mother knows for sure!' or 'So natural, only her mother knows for sure'. She felt she might have to change 'mother' to 'hairdresser' so as not to offend beauty salons. First reaction was that the double meaning in the words would have the line rejected out of hand. Indeed, *Life* magazine would not take the ad. But subsequent research at *Life* failed to find a single female staff member who admitted seeing a double-meaning in it, and the phrases were locked into the form they had for the next eighteen years. ('J' underlines the double-meaning implicit in the slogan with this comment from *The Sensuous Woman*: 'Our world has changed. It's no longer a question of "Does she or doesn't she?" We all know she wants to, is about to, or does.' A New York graffito, quoted 1974: 'Only *his* hairdresser knows for sure.')

Does she...or doesn't she?

Then came **Is She ... Or Isn't She?**   Harmony hair-spray; UK, current 1980. Not by Shirley Polykoff, but a deliberate echo. 'Harmony has a ultra-fine spray to leave hair softer and more natural. She *is* wearing a hairspray but with Harmony it's so fine you're the only one that knows for sure.'

Going! Going!! Gone!!! Too Late for Herpicide   Newbro's Herpicide; US, current from *c.* 1900. Coined by Dr Newbro for his dandruff germ remedy. Accompanied by the cartoon logo of a man looking at the hairs coming out on his comb.

Friday Night Is Amami Night   Amami hair products; UK, current 1920s. (Presumably this inspired the title of the long-running BBC radio show *Friday Night is Music Night*.)

Is It True ... Blondes Have More Fun?   Lady Clairol; US, from 1957. Chosen from ten suggestions, including 'Is it true that blondes are never lonesome?' and 'Is it true blondes marry millionaires?', 'Blondes have more fun' entered the language. The TV jingle even became a hit in the USSR *c.* 1965. Shirley Polykoff, again.

A Little Dab'll Do Ya   Brylcreem; US, from 1949.

Which Twin Has The Toni?   Toni home perms; US, current 1951. A headline that asks a question, a slogan that contains the brand name, and an idea that was dotty enough to be much copied. The ads featured pairs of identical twins (real ones), who also toured doing promotional work for the product. One had a Toni home perm, the other a more expensive perm – a footnote explained which was which. (During the 1970 UK general election, the Liberal Party produced a poster carrying pictures of Harold Wilson and Edward Heath and the slogan **Which Twin Is The Tory?**)

only **LIBERAL** means **PROGRESS**

HAPPY MOTORING

Ask The Man Who Owns One Packard; US, from 1902. This slogan originated with James Ward Packard, the founder of the company, and appeared for many years in all Packard advertising and sales material. Someone had written asking for more information about his motors. Packard told his secretary: 'Tell him that we have no literature – we aren't that big yet – but if he wants to know how good an automobile the Packard is, tell him to ask the man who owns one.' A 1903 placard is the first printed evidence of the slogan's use. It lasted for more than thirty-five years.

At 60 Miles An Hour The Loudest Noise In This New Rolls-Royce Comes From The Electric Clock Rolls-Royce; US, from 1958. The best-known promotional line there has ever been for an automobile. It was not devised by some copywriting genius but came from a car test of the 1958 Silver Cloud by the Technical Editor of *The Motor* magazine. Ogilvy recalls presenting the headline to a senior Rolls-Royce executive in New York who shook his head sadly and said: 'We really ought to do something about that damned clock.' R-R originally used the description **The Best Car In The World** (current 1929).

The Esso Sign Means Happy Motoring Esso; UK, current 1950s. The line occurred in the 1950s' 'longest-running jingle', written by David Bernstein at McCann-Erickson.

Eye It – Try It – Buy It! Chevrolet; US, current 1940.

Fit Dunlop And Be Satisfied Dunlop tyres; UK, quoted 1925.

The Getaway People National Benzole; UK, from 1963. Bryan Oakes of London Press Exchange commented: 'They were the jet set, clean-limbed beautiful girls, the gods and goddesses who did exotic things. We used expensive cars – E-type Jaguars and Aston Martins – and the promise was that, if you get this petrol, you're aligning yourself with those wonderful people, midnight drives on the beach and so on. Of course, it's tough luck – you don't happen to have a Jag just yet, or a girl like that, but any day now ...' (Pearson)

"ASK THE MAN WHO OWNS ONE"

"At 60 miles an hour the loudest noise in this new Rolls-Royce comes from the electric clock"

Go Well – Go Shell   Shell; UK, current from late 1940s, with the follow-on line **Keep Going Well – Keep Going Shell**. Both were featured in early TV commercials, most notably with Bing Crosby singing the jingle in 1962 and Sammy Davis junior in 1964.

Grace ... Space ... Pace   Jaguar; UK, current 1960s.

I Can Be Very Friendly   Sun Oil; US, from 1973. Jane Maas records: 'The chairman and founder of Wells, Rich, Greene, Mary Lawrence, is responsible for the line "I Can Be Very Friendly". During the gasoline crisis, when everyone (customers and dealers) were grouchy about no supplies and long waiting lines, this campaign showed the Sun Oil dealers declaring their intent to win customers over with extra care, concern and good will. It was summed up in the slogan which not only changed the image of Sun Oil in customers' eyes, but also motivated the Sun dealers to be, indeed, very friendly.'

I Told 'Em, Oldham   Oldham car batteries; UK, current late 1950s. Created by Joan Bakewell.

King Of The Road   Lucas cycle lamps and batteries; UK, current 1920s.

Look At All Three!   Chrysler Plymouth; US, from 1932. J. V. Tarleton, of J. Stirling Getchell Inc., recalled: 'The one big fact that gave rise to the whole "Look at all three" idea was that Henry Ford, whose plants had been out of production for almost a year while he tooled up production of the new V-8, was planning to introduce this radically new model in the very same week when Mr Chrysler was planning to announce his new Plymouth ... Getchell and a writer proceeded to bat their brains out for a day or two looking for a unique and different way of announcing a new car – a way that would take advantage of the suspenseful situation created by Mr Ford and get Plymouth through the swinging door on his push ... One of their advertisements showed a large picture of Mr Chrysler in a very informal pose with his foot on the bumper of a new Plymouth. The headline on this ad had originally read "Look at all three low priced cars before you buy." In the process of making the layout, the writer had boiled this down to four big words, "Look At All Three" ... The day when [it] was published in newspapers all over the country, the reaction was unmistakable. Chrysler Corporation dealers reported that their doors started swinging early in the morning and didn't stop until late at night. Plymouth, over night, had become a real contender in the low-priced field.'

Put A Tiger In Your Tank   Esso; US, from 1964. This was a slogan that really took off and gave rise to endless jokes and cartoons. I can remember taking part in a revue sketch about Noah's Ark at Oxford in 1965, the sole purpose of which seemed to be to lead up to the punch line, 'Put A Tiger In Your Tank'. The Esso Tiger had been around in the US and UK a long time before this, however. He first appeared on a poster for Esso Extra in the UK in 1952, realistic, fierce and far from friendly. In 1959 he reappeared in more human form in the US. The line 'Put A Tiger In Your Tank' was thrown away. In 1964, the cartoon tiger was launched in the US, a year later in the UK, and it became a national craze, with countless tiger tails adorning the petrol caps of the nation's cars. Subsequently, he went abroad: 'Mettez un tigre dans votre moteur' appeared in France; in Germany, 'Pack den Tiger in den tank'. In the US, particularly, he gave rise to numerous tiger derivatives. A sample: 'If You Feel Like A Tiger Is In Your Throat Reach For Guardets Lozenges . . .'. A hamburger stand advertised: 'Put A Tiger In Your Tummy.' Tiger Beer in the Japanese *Times* sloganned: 'Put A Tiger In Your Tankard.' Standard Rochester Beer countered: 'Put A Tankard In Your Tiger.' The UK campaign ran for two years before it flagged, hence:

Save The Esso Tiger Esso; UK, from 1967. Dennis Page recalls how he was hired to revive the tiger. He told *Campaign* (7 November 1980): 'I had the ad manager on television advertising the end of the Esso tiger and the tiger saying he was not going to go. Far from saving the tiger, it actually hastened his demise [in 1968].'

Safety Fast MG Motors; UK, current before the Second World War.

Standard Of The World Cadillac; US, current 1912. Created by MacManus, John & Adams (Detroit), the copy ran: 'You know it to be true – you know that the Cadillac is a criterion wherever motor cars are discussed . . . all the Cadillac arguments we could advance in a score of announcements would not be one-hundredth part as impressive as the positive knowledge you hold in your mind at this moment. You know that the Cadillac is *in very fact* the standard of the world. What more is there to be said?'

That's Shell – That Was! Shell; UK, current from late 1930s. A one-headed man with the slogan 'That's Shell – That Is', current in 1929, was developed into a two-headed man with the more widely known slogan. A possibly apocryphal story is that the two-headed man was devised by a member of the public called Horsfield, who received £100 for his trouble.

Think Small Volkswagen; US, from *c.* 1959. Created at Doyle, Dane, Bernbach, this slogan led to the connection between DDB and the Democratic Party. It is said that John F. Kennedy had enjoyed the 'Think Small' campaign – it appealed to his sense of humour – and he suggested the link-up.

PUT A TIGER IN YOUR TANK

Esso EXTRA

NEW POWER-FORMULA ESSO EXTRA BOOSTS POWER THREE WAYS...

1. QUICK STARTING. New Esso Extra gives quick starting, in summer and winter, and *smooth controlled power* with that extra acceleration when you need it.

2. SMOOTH FIRING. Esso Extra's new Power formula improves ignition, helps your engine to fire smoothly and efficiently.

3. HIGH QUALITY. New Esso Extra has the high quality that modern cars need for peak performance. *So call at the Esso sign and fill up with new Esso Extra —and feel the difference.* PUT A TIGER IN YOUR TANK.

Happy Motoring! Esso

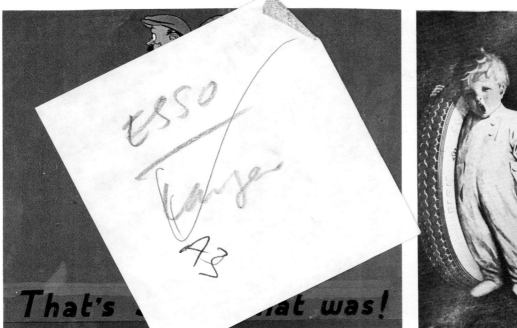

Time To Re-Tire Fisk Rubber Co. tyres; US, from 1907. Burr Griffin did the original sketch for the long-running pun of an ad which showed a yawning child with candle, night-shirt, and tyre. The original slogan was **When It's Time To Re-Tire, Buy A Fisk**.

Watch The Fords Go By Ford Motor Co.; US, from 1908. Started off as a baseball cry in support of the team at the company's Highland Park factory. Applied to ads upon the introduction of the Model T.

When Better Automobiles Are Built ... Buick Will Build Them Buick; US, current 1923.

When You're Only No. 2, You Try Harder. Or Else Avis Rent-A-Car; US, from 1963. Avis had been in the red for fifteen years when, in 1962, Doyle, Dane, Bernbach were hired to do its advertising. A $3 million loss in 1962 became a $3 million profit in 1963, despite warnings that admitting you were not No. 1 was 'un-American' and would merely provide Hertz with a free advertisement.

Where The Rubber Meets The Road Firestone tyres; US, quoted 1976.

You Can Be Sure Of Shell Shell; UK, from *c*. 1931.

You Can Trust Your Car To The Man Who Wears The Star Texaco; US, current 1961.

63

TEETH 'N' SMILES

Cleaning your teeth is not all that a toothpaste does for you. Name the brands supported by the following lines. The answers are on the opposite page.

1. **For People Who Can't Brush Their Teeth After Every Meal**
2. **You'll Wonder Where The Yellow Went**
3. **Did You ********** Your Teeth Today?**
4. **Cleans Your Breath While It Cleans Your Teeth**
5. **The Toothpaste For Thinking People**
6. **Gets Rid Of Film On Teeth**
7. **It's Tingling Fresh**
8. **Looks Like Fun, Cleans Like Crazy**

ANSWERS

1   Gleem; US, quoted 1957. Research showed that many people felt guilty about not brushing their teeth after every meal. So a slogan was coined which gave these people the perfect excuse not to do so.

2   **When You Brush Your Teeth With Pepsodent**; US, current 1950s. An appeal to vanity rather than health.

3   **Did You Maclean Your Teeth Today?**; US, current 1934.

4   Colgate Dental Cream; US, current 1946. Every toothpaste can do it but no one had made it a claim before. Also **The Colgate Ring Of Confidence**.

5   Pebeco; US, current 1931.

6   Pepsodent; US, current early twentieth century. Another of Claude C. Hopkins's great coups – to claim something that every toothpaste could claim and get away with it. He said: 'People do not want to read of penalties. They want to be told of rewards . . . People want to be told the ways to happiness and cheer . . . I resolved to advertise this toothpaste as a creator of beauty.'

7   Gibbs S.R. toothpaste; UK, current 1955. 'It's fresh as ice, it's Gibbs S.R. toothpaste, the tingling fresh toothpaste that does your gums good, too. The tingle you get when you brush with S.R. is much more than a nice taste. It's a tingle of health. It tells you something very important. That you're doing your gums good and toughening them to resist infection. . . .' – accompanied by the visual of a tube embedded in a block of ice, this was the first commercial ever shown on British TV, in 1955.

8   Stripe toothpaste; US, quoted 1958. A man who had invented a tube nozzle which coloured the sides of the emerging ribbon of toothpaste was discovered by J. Walter Thompson in New York. Copywriters picked the name 'Stripe' and coined the slogan, then took the package to Lever Brothers, who found themselves with a ready-made product – a complete reversal of the usual process. (Mayer)

I'M BACKING BRITAIN

However you phrase them – **Made In England**, **British Made** or **Buy British** – appeals to patriotism in advertising have had a rough ride and a limited response. Swan Vesta matches were using the slogan **Support Home Industries** as long ago as 1905. There was a campaign dedicated to the idea of buying British goods in preference to others in the wake of the First World War – part of an effort to revive British trade. But, as a commentator wrote in 1925: 'The slogan has never from its birth rung like true metal. There is nothing satisfying about it. It savours of a cry of distress – an S.O.S. – and does not begin to represent the spirit of a commerce that is reconstructing itself and paying its debts simultaneously.'

Somehow, patriotism (which can be appealed to legitimately in time of war) does not mix with commerce. Besides, there is a suspicion of boycott about such phrases. There is also the obstacle of identification – how does the consumer *know* what is British and what is not? How can he make the choice when he does not know what component parts are used in making a product?

All this has not prevented such slogans reappearing whenever things have looked bleak for the economy. **British Is Best** has been used at regular chauvinistic intervals. The most curious revival of the 'Buy British' theme was in January 1968 when, in the wake of the Labour Government's decision to devalue the pound sterling, all kinds of peculiar reactions filled the air. Valerie, Brenda, Joan, Carol and Christine – typists at the Colt Heating and Ventilation offices at Surbiton – responded to a Christmas message from their boss to make some special work-effort. From 1 January they declared they would work half an hour extra each day for no extra pay. Was this spontaneous, or were they pushed? Whatever the case, the media leapt in. The slogan **I'm Backing Britain** appeared from somewhere and Prime Minister Harold Wilson said, 'What we want is "Back Britain", not back-biting.' The Industrial Society launched an official campaign on 24 January. Bruce Forsyth recorded a song 'I'm Backing Britain'. Two million badges and stickers were manufactured. A press ad listed 'three things retired folk could do' to help the economy or 'seven things a manufacturer could do'. People actually started sending money to the Chancellor of the Exchequer. It was as barmy as that. Then things turned sour.

'Back Britain' T-shirts were found to have been made in Portugal. Trade unions objected to the idea of anyone working extra hours for no more pay. A rival 'Help Britain' group led by Robert Maxwell MP conflicted with the Industrial Society's effort. The whole thing had fizzled out by August.

IN THIS STYLE 10/6

The price-ticket on the Mad Hatter's hat in the Tenniel illustration for Lewis Carroll's *Alice's Adventures In Wonderland* (ten shillings and sixpence being the equivalent of $52\frac{1}{2}$p in post-1971 British currency) introduces a selection of fictional slogans – or perhaps one should say 'slogans in fiction', because some of them are quite convincing ...

'P.P.' What About You?   In *Keep The Aspidistra Flying*, George Orwell describes an advertising campaign by the Queen of Sheba Toilet Requisites Co. for the deodorant, 'April Dew'. The firm was after a phrase like 'Night Starvation' that would 'rankle in the public consciousness like a poisoned arrow'. The idea of smelly feet becomes 'Pedic Perspiration' or 'P.P.'

All Animals Are Equal, But Some Animals Are More Equal Than Others

Napoleon Is Always Right

Vote For Snowball And The Three Day Week

Vote For Napoleon And The Full Manger
from Animal Farm by George Orwell

Big Brother Is Watching You

Freedom Is Slavery

Ignorance Is Strength

War Is Peace

from *Nineteen Eighty-Four* by George Orwell

If You Ain't Eatin' Wham
You Ain't Eatin' Ham
In the film *Mr Blandings Builds His Dream House*, Cary Grant portrays an advertising man in search of a slogan which eludes him until his black cook utters these immortal words.

It's A Far, Far Butter Thing ...
A suggested slogan for margarine from *Murder Must Advertise* by Dorothy L. Sayers. The whole of this novel (1933) is set in Pym's, an advertising agency modelled on the firm of S. H. Benson, where Sayers worked in the 1920s and 1930s. The book positively teems with suggested and mostly rejected advertising lines – some devised by Lord Peter Wimsey himself, disguised as Death Bredon, a trainee copywriter:

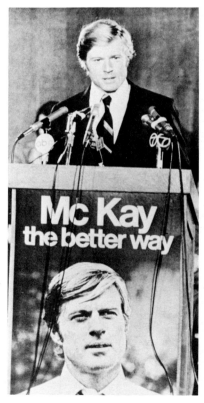

Bigger And Butter Value For Money

You'd Be Ready To Bet It Was Butter

If You Kept A Cow In The Kitchen You Could Get No Better Bread-Spread Than G. P. Margarine

Don't Say Soap, Say Sopo!

Makes Monday, Fun-Day

Are You A Whiffler? If Not, Why Not?

It Isn't Dear, It's Darling

Everyone Everywhere Always Agrees
On The Flavour And Value Of Twentyman's Teas

McKay: The Better Way
Robert Redford won on this slogan in the film *The Candidate*. It caught only too well the uninspired quality of most modern political slogans.

KIKES, KOONS, AND KATHOLICS

Popular protest – for and against – kikes (Jews), black people, and other vocal minorities and causes in the UK and the US:

When Adam Delved And Eve Span, Who Was Then A Gentleman? A rhyme from the Peasants' Revolt, 1381. Taken as the text for a sermon preached by John Ball to Wat Tyler's men at Blackheath.

No Popery, No Tyranny, No Wooden Shoes Defoe said that there were a hundred thousand fellows in his time ready to fight to the death against popery, without knowing whether popery was a man or a horse. After the initial impact of the Restoration had worn off, this was the cry that came to be heard. The wife of Charles II, Catherine of Braganza, was a Roman Catholic and so was his brother (later James II). They were surrounded by priests and the Fire of London (1666) was put down to papist action and foreign interference. Hence, the anti-Roman Catholicism of the slogan coupled with general English distrust of foreigners (wooden shoes=French *sabots*). The variation **No Jews – No Wooden Shoes** (obvious rhyming slang) occurred in 1753 when an anti-Jewish Bill was before Parliament.

The cry 'No Popery' is chiefly associated, however, with the Gordon Riots of 1780, when Lord George Gordon fomented a violent protest against legislation which had lightened penalties on Roman Catholics. The riots in London were put down by George III's troops (and form the background to Charles Dickens's novel *Barnaby Rudge*). The slogan was again used by supporters of the Duke of Portland's government opposed to Catholic Emancipation, in 1807.

Wilkes And Liberty Cry of the London mob, 1764, in support of John Wilkes (1727–97), the radical politician, who was repeatedly elected to Parliament despite ministerial attempts to exclude him because of his scurrilous attacks on the government. He was a popular champion of parliamentary reform and of the cause of the colonies in the War of American Independence.

One Man, One Vote A phrase first coined in the nineteenth century for a campaign led by Major John Cartwright (1740–1824), a radical MP ('The Father of Reform'), in the fight against plural voting. It was possible in those days for a man to cast two votes, one on the basis of residence and the other by virtue of business or university qualifications. This right was not abolished until 1948. The phrase arose again during the period of the illegal Unilateral Declaration of Independence in Rhodesia (1965–80) to indicate a basic condition required by the British government before the breakaway could be legitimised. The phrase has also been used in the US, in civil rights contexts.

Home Rule (For Ever) First used about 1860 in its usual sense of home rule for Ireland, then under British rule. The Home Rule Movement led by Sinn Fein ultimately led to the founding of the Irish Free State – with Northern Ireland remaining part of the UK.

Ulster Will Fight, And Ulster Will Be Right In an open letter to a Liberal-Unionist in May 1886, Lord Randolph Churchill wrote: 'Ulster will not be a consenting party; Ulster at the proper moment will resort to a supreme arbitrament of force; Ulster will fight and Ulster will be right.' Taken up by Ulster Volunteers, loyal to the British Crown, and opposing Irish Home Rule, 1913–14.

The Saloon Must Go Anti-Saloon League, founded in 1893. When saloons were a proliferating, noisy, smelly nuisance, the League used political pressure to bring the temperance movement to a successful climax in Prohibition.

Kill The Kikes, Koons, And Katholics Ku Klux Klan, from the late nineteenth century.

Bring Back The Cat The cat-o'-nine-tails was the nine-thong whip once used to enforce discipline in the Royal Navy. This phrase has long been the cry of corporal punishment enthusiasts demanding its return. Usually associated with right-wing 'hangers and floggers' within the Conservative Party.

Not A Penny Off The Pay, Not A Minute On The Day (and variants) Coined by A. J. Cook, Secretary of the Union of Mineworkers, and used in the run-up to the miners' strike of 1926 (which led to the General Strike). (Compare:

> In his chamber, weak and dying
> While the Norman Baron lay,
> Loud, without, his men were crying
> 'Shorter hours and better pay.'
> *Anon.*)

You Gave Us Beer, Now Give Us Water Dustbowl farmers' plea (US), 1933. The year of the great drought, which destroyed crops and created dust-storms was, ironically, when Prohibition ended.

A Vote For Hogg Is A Vote For Hitler A famous by-election took place at Oxford in the month after the Munich agreement in 1938. Quintin Hogg (later Lord Hailsham) stood as the champion of Munich and the Prime Minister, Neville Chamberlain; A. D. Lindsay, Master of Balliol and a member of the Labour Party, stood as a representative of the anti-fascist Popular Front. Hogg won.

Ban The Bomb One of the simplest and best-known alliterative slogans, current in the US from 1953 and marginally later in the UK. The Campaign for Nuclear Disarmament was not publicly launched until February 1958. (Richard Crossman refers to 'Scrap the Bomb' in a 1957 press article.)

Better Red Than Dead   A slogan of the British nuclear disarmament movement. Bertrand Russell wrote in 1958: 'If no alternative remains except communist domination or the extinction of the human race, the former alternative is the lesser of two evils' – hence the slogan. The counter-cry **Better Dead Than Red** became almost equally well established.

Marples Must Go   Ernest Marples (1907–78) was the hyperactive Conservative Minister of Transport (1959–64). This slogan first arose in October 1962 (and was quoted as such in a *Daily Herald* headline) after he had intervened in the build-up to the publication of the Beeching Report, which recommended sweeping cuts in rail services. 'Trades union leaders and Labour MPs have started a Marples Must Go campaign,' the *Herald* reported, 'convinced that Marples must be sacked to save a head-on clash between railway unions and government.' When the report was finally published in March 1963, Marples was judged to have given a poor defence of it in the House of Commons.

However, it was because of motoring matters that the slogan was taken up at a more popular level. Marples had already introduced Britain to parking zones, car tests, and panda crossings. He could claim that London's traffic was moving $37\frac{1}{2}$ per cent faster as a result of his draconian measures. But many saw them as an infringement of individual liberty. In May 1963, Marples introduced 'totting up' for motoring convictions and, shortly afterwards, a 50 m.p.h. speed limit at peak summer weekends in an effort to reduce the number of road accidents. It was this last measure that produced a rash of car stickers bearing this cry. It appeared daubed on a bridge over the M1 motorway in August.

When Barbara Castle became Labour Transport Minister in 1965 and introduced breath-tests to combat drunken driving, car stickers appeared saying 'Marples Come Back, All Is Forgiven.'

If You Want A Nigger For A Neighbour – Vote Labour   appeared in one constituency – Smethwick – during the 1964 UK general election. The seat was won from Labour by Peter Griffiths, later described by the incoming Prime Minister, Harold Wilson, as 'a member who, until another election returns him to oblivion, will serve his time here as a parliamentary leper'.

Hearts And Minds   The Vietnam War (*c.* 1959–73) produced almost no patriotic American slogans – reflecting the mixed support for an unpopular and ultimately unsuccessful operation. 'Hearts And Minds', meaning what had to be won, was a slogan of sorts for the US government. Its origins go back to Theodore Roosevelt's day when Douglas MacArthur, as a young aide, asked him in 1906 to what he attributed his popularity. The President replied: 'To put into words what is in their hearts and minds but not in their mouths.' (Safire)

A ribald Green Beret use of the phrase could be observed during the war above the bar in the den of Charles W. Colson (later indicted over the Watergate cover-up): **If You Got 'Em By The Balls, Their Hearts And Minds Will Follow**.

Abolish The Draft and **Hell, No, We Won't Go** US anti-draft slogans, 1960s.

America, Love It Or Leave It The most memorable of the few patriotic slogans, current from 1969.

Make Love, Not War A 'peacenik' and 'flower power' sentiment expressed from the mid-1960s, not just applied to Vietnam. It was written up in English at the University of Nanterre during the French student revolution of May 1968.

Turn On, Tune In, Drop Out Hippie slogan and LSD motto associated with Dr Timothy Leary, from *c.* 1967.

Peace Now On poster, quoted 1968 – echoing the 'now' theme also used in civil rights slogans.

Build Not Burn Students For A Democratic Society, late 1960s.

Flower Power Hippie slogan, 1960s, inspired no doubt by 'Black Power'. Flowers were used as a love symbol.

Shoot To Live The Weathermen (militant revolutionary group), *c.* 1969.

Support Your Local Police, Keep Them Independent Police bumper sticker, 1969. The film *Support Your Local Sheriff* had appeared in 1968, but the idea of supporting or consulting your local or neighbourhood whatever was already well established.

Out Of The Closets And Into The Streets Gay Liberation Front, *c.* 1969.

Say It Loud, We're Gay And We're Proud Gay Liberation Front.

**2-4-6-8,
Gay Is Just As Good As Straight
3-5-7-9
Lesbians Are Mighty Fine** Gay Liberation Front, 1970s.

Register Communists Not Guns John Birch Society, 1970.

Guns Don't Kill People, People Kill People National Rifle Association, current 1981.

YOUR OWN, YOUR VERY OWN

A phrase describing the nature of their act was a distinctive feature of billing for music-hall and variety artists in the UK and vaudeville performers in the US. At times, such 'bill matter' was used as more than a tag. As an up-and-coming comedian, Tommy Trinder bought space on hoardings all over London to proclaim: **If It's Laughter You're After, Trinder's The Name**.

Al Jolson

The World's Greatest Entertainer	Al Jolson
The Man With The Golden Trumpet	Eddie Calvert
Creating An Impression	Peter Cavanagh
The One And Only	Phyllis Dixey
A Song, A Smile, And A Piano	Norman Long
The Human Hairpin	Carlton
The Wigan Nightingale	George Formby senior
Fiddling And Fooling	Ted Ray
The Essence of Eccentricity	Nellie Wallace
America's Beloved Baritone	John Charles Thomas
The Velvet Fog	Mel Torme
The Singer With The Smile In His Voice	Jack Smith
Almost A Gentleman	Billy Bennett
The Casual Comedian	Geep Martin (*whose hands shook so much you could hear his script rattling at the microphone*)
The Cheeky Chappie	Max Miller
The Chocolate Coloured Coon	G. H. Elliott
The Last Of The Red Hot Mamas	Sophie Tucker (*from the title of a song by Jack Yellen, introduced by her in 1928*)
The Prime Minister Of Mirth	George Robey
She's No Lady!	George Lacy (*female impersonator*)
The Long And The Short Of It	Ethel Revnel and Gracie West

Max Miller

The Man With The Orchid-Lined Voice	Enrico Caruso (*coined by his publicist, Edward L. Bernays*)
Two Ton Tessie	Tessie O'Shea
The Girl Who Made Vaudeville Famous	Eva Tanguay
Radio's Bouncing Czech	Egon Regon
A Concert-in-a Act	Peter and Mary Honri
Fills The Stage With Flags	Kardomah
The Clown Prince Of Wales	Wyn Calvin
Oh No, There Isn't!	The Two Pirates
Britain's Favourite American Performers/America's Favorite British Performers	Kimberly & Page (*in UK and US*)
Too Mean To Tell You What They Do	The Three Aberdonians

Sophie Tucker

LET'S MAKE AMERICA GREAT AGAIN

American presidential elections have given rise to some of the quirkiest political slogans and, increasingly of late, to some of the dullest. 'Let's Make America Great Again', for example, has been used more than once and could apply to any candidate, Democratic or Republican, incumbent or challenger. Here, taken from some of the past campaigns, are the more pointed rallying cries, both official and unofficial:

1828 **Bargain And Corruption** No one candidate in the previous election had received a majority of the electoral vote although Andrew Jackson was in the lead. When the election came to be decided by the House of Representatives, John Quincy Adams struck a deal with fellow candidate Henry Clay (Speaker of the House) by which Adams won and Clay became Secretary of State. In 1828, using the slogan 'Bargain And Corruption', Jackson unseated President Adams.

1840 **Tippecanoe And Tyler Too** 'Tippecanoe' refers to General William Henry Harrison, the Whig candidate, who had defeated Indians at Tippecanoe Creek in 1811. John Tyler stood as Vice-President. The Democrats renominated President Van Buren and characterised Harrison as the 'Log Cabin And Hard Cider' candidate – a challenge the Whigs turned to their advantage by forming log cabin clubs and serving hard cider at rallies. Van Buren, in turn, was characterised as an effete New Yorker drinking wine from 'coolers of silver', and acquired the nickname 'Old Kinderhook' from the name of his birthplace in New York State. **O.K.** became a slogan in the 1840 campaign, too, adding to the colourful etymology of that phrase. It was not O.K. for Van Buren, however – he was unseated.

1844 **Who's Polk?** James K. Polk, the first 'dark horse' candidate, took the Democratic nomination from ex-President Van Buren. As a compromise candidate he was little known (just as more than a century later Jimmy Carter initially gave rise to the cry 'Jimmy Who?'). He campaigned with the expansionist slogan **54–40 Or Fight**, seeking to reoccupy the territory of Oregon, then jointly held by Britain and the US, up to a northern boundary with Canada at 54° 40'. The Democrats won the election but President Polk negotiated a compromise settlement at the 49th Parallel. Coinage of the phrase is credited to Samuel Medary, an editor from Ohio, though William Allen, a Democratic Senator from that state, used it in a speech before the US Senate.

1852 **We Polked You in 1844, We Shall Pierce You In 1852** The next 'dark horse' was Franklin Pierce, who was not considered as the Democrats' candidate until the 35th ballot at the party convention. When he was selected on the 49th, the slogan was inevitable. He won the election, too.

James K. Polk

1856 **Free Soil, Free Men, Free Speech, Frémont** The new Republican Party's first candidate was John C. Frémont, a soldier and explorer. When formed two years before, the party had absorbed abolitionists including the Free Soil Party (which was dedicated to free land for settlers as well as to the abolition of slavery) who used the slogan **Free Soil, Free Speech, Free Labour, And Free Men**, which the Republicans adapted. Meanwhile, the American (Know Nothing) Party which supported ex-President Fillmore in the race used the slogan **Peace At Any Price** to mean that they were willing to accept slavery for blacks in order to avoid a civil war. This phrase had been coined in 1848 by the French foreign affairs minister, Alphonse de Lamartine. Neither Frémont nor Fillmore won. James Buchanan did.

1872 **Anything To Beat Grant** After only one term it was apparent that President Grant, though a war hero, was unsuited to the presidency. The Liberal Republican Party emerged to unseat him with Horace Greeley as candidate – but failed to do so.

1876 **Hayes, Hard Money And Hard Times** A Democratic challenge to the Republican candidate Rutherford B. Hayes, who won after a disputed election.

1884 **Rum, Romanism, Rebellion** Samuel Dickinson Burchard, speaking on behalf of clergymen who supported the Republican candidate, James G. Blaine, said: 'We are Republicans, and don't propose to leave our party and identify ourselves with the party whose antecedents have been Rum, Romanism, and Rebellion.' His Irish-Catholic audience in New York took none too kindly to this. Blaine lost the state's vote, and the presidency, to Grover Cleveland.

1900 **Full Dinner Pail** A Republican phrase which helped secure the re-election of President McKinley. Prosperity of this type was plainly more appealing to the average voter than William Jennings Bryan's call for 'Immediate Freedom For The Philippines'. A remark made by McKinley supporter Senator Mark Hanna, 'We Will Stand Pat', gave rise to the idea that 'Stand Pat With McKinley' was used as a slogan in this election but this appears to be a fallacy.

1904 **You Can't Beat Somebody With Nobody** And President Theodore Roosevelt was re-elected over the Democratic challenger Alton B. Parker.

1916 **He Kept Us Out Of War** and **Wilson's Wisdom Wins Without War** Woodrow Wilson's slogans for re-election were true at the time (although he had nothing to do with them) but he took the US into the First World War the following year.

1920 **Back To Normalcy** and **Return To Normalcy With Harding** were used effectively in the Republican campaign which took Warren G. Harding to the White House. Both were based on his remark of that year: 'America's present need is not heroics but healing, not nostrums but normalcy.'

1924 **Keep Cool With Coolidge** and **Coolidge Or Chaos** Calvin C. Coolidge had assumed the presidency in 1923 on the death of Harding. He won this election by a wide margin.

1928 **Hoover And Happiness, Or Smith And Soup Houses** Herbert Hoover easily defeated the Democrat Alfred E. Smith in the prosperous calm before the economic storm. 'Two Chickens For Every Pot' is said, erroneously, to have been used by Hoover in the campaign. The suggestion appears to have arisen because Smith mocked a Republican flysheet headed 'A Chicken in Every Pot' – using the phrase coined by King Henry IV of France (1553–1610) when he said: 'I wish that there would not be a peasant so poor in all my realm who would not have a chicken in his pot every Sunday.'

1932 **In Hoover We Trusted, Now We Are Busted** After the stock-market and financial crash, Hoover was roundly defeated by the Democratic challenger Franklin D. Roosevelt.

1936 **Land Landon With A Landslide** and **Land A Job With Landon** Roosevelt's New Deal policies were challenged by the Republican Governor, Alfred M. Landon. Telephone operators at the switchboard of the *Chicago Tribune* answered calls with 'Only X more days to **Save The American Way Of Life**.' Democrats encouraged the incumbent to **Carry On, Roosevelt**. He did.

1940 **We Want Wilkie** At the Republican convention, the balconies were packed with supporters of Wendell Wilkie. They helped sway the nomination in his direction. 'Win With Wilkie' did not help unseat FDR. The President had his own slogan for crowd repetition: **Martin, Barton And Fish**. Seeking to blame Republicans for US military unpreparedness, he cited three Congressmen – Joseph Martin, Bruce Barton (later of the advertising firm, Batten, Barton, Durstine & Osborn), and Hamilton Fish. The speech in which the phrase arose was written by Judge Samuel I. Rosenman and Robert E. Sherwood, the dramatist. Crowds loved to join in the rhythmic line echoing 'Wynken, Blynken and Nod'.

1944 **Time For A Change** Twelve years of FDR led to his Republican challenger, Thomas E. Dewey, saying: 'That's why it's time for a change.' But the call was ignored, as it was when he repeated it four years later. It was finally effective for the Republicans in 1952.

1948 **Don't Let Them Take It Away** Fears that a Republican president might re-enter the White House after sixteen years of Democratic rule gave rise to this unofficial slogan. It worked this time for Harry S. Truman's election but not when the slogan was revived in 1952. At the beginning of the 1948 campaign Truman told Alben Barkley, his running mate, 'I'm going to fight hard. I'm going to give them hell.' So **Give 'Em Hell, Harry** became a battle-cry.

1952 **I Like Ike** This slogan began appearing on buttons in 1947 as the Second World War general, Dwight David Eisenhower, began to be spoken of as a possible presidential nominee (initially as a Democrat). By 1950 Irving Berlin was including one of his least notable songs, 'They Like Ike', in *Call Me Madam* and 15,000 people at a rally in Madison Square Gardens were urging Eisenhower to return from his military sojourn in Paris and run as a Republican in 1952, with the chant 'We Like Ike'. It worked. The three sharp monosyllables and the effectiveness of the repeated 'i' sound in 'I Like Ike' made it an enduring slogan throughout the fifties. A sign observed during the 1960 campaign said 'We Like Ike But We Back Jack.' K_1C_2 or **Korea, Communism And Corruption** was the hard-hitting slogan of the 1952 campaign, representing the three charges against the incumbent Democrats – that they were unable to end the war, were soft on communism, and had created a mess in Washington. **I Shall Go To Korea** was an Eisenhower promise made in a campaign speech. **Had Enough?** pointed up the Republicans' long absence from power. **You Never Had It So Good** was a Democratic slogan which failed to deliver for Adlai Stevenson.

1960 **Let's Get America Moving Again** (John F. Kennedy) and **Keep The Peace Without Surrender** (Richard M. Nixon) were interchangeable slogans from the election that JFK won.

1964 **All The Way With LBJ** and **USA For LBJ** were employed by Lyndon B. Johnson in the election that gave him a landslide victory over the Republican, Barry M. Goldwater, in the year following the Kennedy assassination. 'All The Way With LBJ' had first been used when Johnson was seeking the presidential nomination which eventually went to Kennedy in 1960. 'All through the fall and winter of 1959 and 1960,' wrote Theodore White, 'the noisemakers of the Johnson campaign ... chanted "All The Way With LBJ" across the South and Far West, instantly identifiable by their Texan garb, their ten-gallon hats (and, said their enemies, the cowflap on their boots).' **In Your Heart You Know I'm/He's Right** was the much-parodied Goldwater slogan – 'In Your Gut You Know He's Nuts'; 'You Know In Your Heart He's Right – Far Right.' **$AuH_2O = 1964$** gave rise to the riposte '$AuH_2O = H_2S$' and 'Goldwater in '64, Hot Water in '65, Bread and Water in '66'.

1968 **Nixon's The One** So, indeed, he was, if his official slogan can be said to have any meaning at all. Later in the campaign there appeared **This Time Vote Like Your Whole Life Depended On It**. Democratic opponent Hubert H. Humphrey countered in vain with **The Politics Of Joy**, and third-party candidate George C. Wallace sniped at the big boys with the charge that there was **Not A Dime's Worth Of Difference**. Nixon won.

1972 **Send Them A Message** George C. Wallace's plea, by which he sought to attract votes away from Nixon and the Democrat George McGovern by pointing up the gulf between the little people in the electorate and the aloof politicians in power, failed to stop Nixon winning again.

1976 **He's Making Us Proud Again** Gerald R. Ford needed to, having assumed the presidency in the wake of Watergate. He was rejected in favour of the Democrat who used the catchphrase/slogan **My Name Is Jimmy Carter And I'm Running For President** as well as the loftier cry, **Why Not The Best?**

1980 **The Time Is Now** Another incontestable statement that helped bring Ronald Reagan to power. His long-time supporters continued to use **Win This One For The Gipper** – a reference to Reagan's earlier existence as a film actor. In *Knute Rockne* he played a football star, George Gipp, who died young. The team's coach sent his team-mates out on to the field with this exhortation. Jimmy Carter's detractors within and without his own party came up with **A.B.C. – Anyone But Carter**.

MAKE BRITAIN GREAT AGAIN

No general election is complete without slogans. Here are some of the more intriguing ones from British Conservative and Labour campaigns:

1923 **Yesterday The Trenches, Today The Unemployed** was used in the aftermath of the First World War and prior to the first Labour election victory, under Ramsay MacDonald.

1929 **Safety First** was a Tory slogan under which Stanley Baldwin fought for re-election. Posters showed the 'wise and honest' face of the Prime Minister, who, inevitably, was smoking a pipe, and the further words: 'Stanley Baldwin, The Man You Can Trust.' He was even shown as a sea-captain, wearing a sou-wester, accompanied by the slogan **Trust Baldwin, He Will Steer You To Safety**. Conservative Central Office had thought that the General Strike of not so long before (1926) called for this reassuring approach but, with growing unemployment and the depression on the way, the slogan proved a loser. The party chairman, J. C. C. Davidson, who had accepted the idea from Benson's agency, took the blame for the Tories' defeat at the hands of Ramsay MacDonald and the Labour Party. The phrase came into use in the 1890s when railway companies maintained that 'the Safety of the Passenger is our First Concern'. In 1916, the London General Bus Company formed a London Safety First Council. The 1922 general election saw the phrase in use as a political slogan for the Conservatives. They subsequently won with it in 1931. In 1934 the National Safety First Association was formed, concerned with road and industrial safety.

1945 **Send Him Back To Finish The Job** Used by Winston Churchill seeking to return as Conservative Prime Minister after his leadership of an all-party War Cabinet. The slogan backfired when it was seen to be supported by those who had tried to keep Churchill out of power in 1940. A Labour victory brought in Clement Attlee as Prime Minister.

1950 **Your Future Is In Your Hands/A Vote For The Liberals Is A Vote Wasted/Make Britain Great Again** led to defeat by a yet smaller margin. The Tories were returned under Churchill the following year.

1959 **Life's Better With The Conservatives – Don't Let Labour Ruin It** A Tory slogan which helped bring them a further period of office after an election in which many broadcasting and advertising techniques were applied to UK politics for the first time. There was much to justify the claim: material conditions had improved for most people; the balance of payments surplus, gold and dollar reserves were at a high level; wages were up; and taxation had gone down. The slogan emerged from consultations between Central Office and the Colman, Prentis & Varley agency. In his book *Influencing Voters*, Richard Rose says he knew of four people who claimed to have originated the slogan. Ronald Simms was the PR chief at Central Office from 1957 to 1967. He is said to have come up with 'Life Is Good With The Conservatives, Don't Let The Socialists Spoil It'. Lord Hailsham wanted 'better' instead of 'good' and CPV changed 'spoil' to 'ruin'. On the other hand, Maurice Smelt writes: 'The slogan was so successful that many people have claimed it (that always happens): but it was just a perfectly routine thing I did one afternoon in 1959, as the copywriter on the Conservative account at CPV. The brief from Oliver Poole was to say something like "You've Never Had It So Good", but with less cynicism and more bite. The first five words were the paraphrase: and the whole ten told what I still think was a truth for its time. It's the slogan I am proudest of.'

As is shown elsewhere, the phrase 'You Never Had It So Good' was used by the Democrats in the 1952 US presidential election. Given the way Harold Macmillan's 'You've Never Had It So Good' came to dog him, it would be surprising if it had been used in any official campaign. The phrase was rejected by the Conservatives' publicity group, partly because it 'violated a basic advertising axiom that statements should be positive, not negative', but it hovered about unofficially, and there was an official poster which came very close with **You're Having It Good, Have It Better**.

1964 **Let's Go With Labour, And We'll Get Things Done** At this election, the Labour Party overcame its earlier inhibitions about bringing in help from the advertising world, as the Conservatives had done for many years. As early as January 1963, Labour's advertising group agreed to use a thumb's-up sign derived from Norman Vaughan, compère of the ITV show *Sunday Night at the London Palladium*. (They shrank, however, from incorporating his catchphrases 'swinging' and 'dodgy' in the slogan 'Tories Dodgy – Labour Swinging' for fear that not all the electorate would know what they were on about.) Anthony Howard and Richard West say in *The Making of the Prime Minister* that 'everybody agreed that the

YESTERDAY'S MEN
(They failed before!)

word "Go" was necessary to the slogan. It implied dynamism and action; it was short and pithy.' Suggestions included 'Labour's Got Go', 'Labour Goes Ahead', 'All Systems Go', 'Labour For Go', and 'Labour's On The Go'. Of this last one, Harold Wilson said that it sounded like 'Labour On The Po' and Percy Clark from Labour Party HQ said that it might sound as if the party had diarrhoea. The group finally hit on its successful slogan and 'Let's Go With Labour' was used for the eighteen months prior to the election. David Kingsley, one of the advertising people involved, says the phrase was coined by Ros Allen. Labour won by a narrow margin.

1966   **You Know Labour Government Works**   After almost four years in power, the Labour Government went to the country in an effort to increase its majority and used a slogan intended to reflect its credibility (it had previously been out of power for thirteen years). David Kingsley says that the slogan was 'largely my own creation but it grew out of team-work with Dennis Lyons and Peter Lovell-Davis'. A version of its creation is that Lovell-Davis suggested 'Labour Government Works' and Kingsley added the 'You Know'.

1970   **Yesterday's Men**   David Kingsley says that this phrase 'came from the three of us in the team and we never could untangle precisely who created it' – perhaps as well, as it had to be dropped for reasons of taste during the campaign. A colour poster showing crudely coloured models of Conservative politicians (Edward Heath, Iain Macleod, Lord Hailsham and others) and the additional line 'They failed before' was felt to 'degrade' politics. Labour lost the election to 'Yesterday's Men' but the phrase continued to cause trouble. In 1971 it was used as the title of a BBC TV programme about the defeated Labour leaders and how they were faring in Opposition. This soured relations between the BBC and the Labour Party for a long time afterwards.

1974   **Britain Will *Win* With Labour**   Used from August onwards in the second election of that year, which secured Labour's majority for a further four and a half years.

1979   **Labour Is The Answer**   Labour lost to the Conservatives under Margaret Thatcher. (A graffito added: 'If Labour is the answer, it's a bloody silly question'.) The Conservative slogan – **Labour Isn't Working – Britain's Better Off With The Conservatives** – first appeared in 1978 on posters showing a long queue outside an employment office. Created by Saatchi & Saatchi, it was later widely used in the campaign that took Margaret Thatcher to Downing Street. When unemployment continued to rise under the Conservatives the poster was recalled with irony. (Rumour has it that there was, briefly, a poster referring to Mrs Thatcher which proclaimed 'Put A Woman On Top For A Change'.)

LIKE MOTHER USED TO MAKE

Drinka Pinta Milka Day UK, from 1958. The target was to get everyone drinking one pint of milk a day and the slogan was a piece of 'bath-tub inspiration' that came from the client, namely Bertrand Whitehead, Executive Officer of the National Milk Publicity Council of England and Wales. Francis Ogilvy, Chairman of Mather & Crowther, apparently insisted on it being used over the protests of the creative department, which wanted it strangled at birth. It was the sort of coinage to drive teachers and pedants to apoplexy, but the 'pinta' achieved its own entry in *Chambers Twentieth Century Dictionary*.

Drink More Milk UK, quoted 1928. A later campaign from the Milk Marketing Board drew a response from the British Medical Association in January 1938 – an ad headed 'Is *All* Milk Safe To Drink?' (suggesting that milk should be tested for tuberculosis). The BMA had to modify this 'knocking copy' to 'Drink Safe Milk'.

Full Of Natural Goodness UK, current 1980.

If It's Borden's, It's *Got* To Be Good US, current 1940s. Used on dairy products from the Borden company and featuring 'Elsie the Cow'.

Milk From Contented Cows US, from 1906. Elbridge A. Stuart was the man who gave rise to Carnation evaporated milk in 1899. Seven years later he went to Chicago to lay on an advertising campaign with the Mahin agency. John Lee Mahin and Stuart, having decided on the main lines of the campaign, called in a new young copywriter called Helen Mar.

'Mr Stuart gave me a description of the conditions under which Carnation was produced,' she recalled many years later. 'In his own sincere and quiet way he spoke of the ever-verdant pastures of Washington and Oregon, where grazed the carefully kept Holstein herds that supplied the raw milk. He described in a manner worthy of Burton Holmes the picturesque background of these pastures from which danced and dashed the pure, sparkling waters to quench the thirst of the herds and render more tender the juicy

grasses they fed on. He spoke of the shade of luxuriant trees under which the herds might rest. Remembering my lectures in medical college and recalling that milk produced in mental and physical ease is more readily digested – I involuntarily exclaimed: "Ah! The milk of contented cows!" Mr Mahin's pencil tapped on the table top and he and Mr Stuart spoke almost together: "That's our slogan."'

And so it has remained – or almost. The words on the can have usually read: 'From Contented Cows'. Later came the jingle:

Carnation Milk is the best in the land,
Here I sit with a can in my hand.
No tits to pull, no hay to pitch –
Just punch a hole in the son of a bitch.

Watch Out There's A Humphrey About   UK, current 1974. The Humphreys were a mythical race supposed to steal milk when nobody was looking. They were not seen (in TV ads) – only the red-striped straws through which they sipped.

GOLDEN MOTTOES IN THE MOUTH*

If a slogan promotes a cause, then mottoes and war-cries can on occasion fulfil the same purpose. The word slogan or 'slug-horn' derives from the Gaelic *sluagh-ghairm*, meaning 'host-cry' or 'army-shout'. The Scottish Home family's famous cry **A Home, A Home, A Home!** not only identified them but spurred the soldiers on to action, despite the legend that on hearing it at the Battle of Flodden Field in 1513 they turned tail and headed for home.

As for the Medicis in Florence, taking their cue from the family arms, their supporters would cry: **Palle, Palle** (which translated means 'Balls, Balls!').

Most mottoes are less aggressive than slogans. Sometimes they are indistinguishable – as with the motto of the Nation Life Assurance company which collapsed in 1974: **Safe And Sure**. From the large number available, here is a small sample of mottoes which have the force of slogans or which just go to show how difficult it is to categorise phrases of this type:

All For One, And One For All ('Tous pour un, un pour tous')   The motto of the fictional Three Musketeers in the novel by Alexandre Dumas.

Be Prepared   The motto of the Boy Scout movement, based on the initials of its founder Sir Robert Baden-Powell. (Also used as an advertising slogan by Pears' Soap.)

Courtesy And Care   The Automobile Association (UK). Devised by Viscount Brentford, chairman, 1910–22. Included in its armorial bearings.

The Difficult We Do Immediately, The Impossible Takes A Little Longer   *Bartlett's Familiar Quotations* attributes this motto, now widespread, to the US Army Service Forces and traces it back to Charles Alexandre De Calonne (1734–1802): 'Madame, si c'est possible, c'est fait; impossible? cela se fera.'

*Herman Melville

Every Day And In Every Way I Am Getting Better And Better (though sometimes found as **Every Day In Every Way . . .** or **Day By Day In Every Way**)   The French psychologist Émile Coué was the originator of a system of 'Self-Mastery Through Conscious Auto-suggestion' which had a brief vogue in the 1920s. His patients had to repeat this phrase over and over and it became a popular catchphrase of the time, though physical improvement did not noticeably follow. Couéism died with its inventor in 1926. (It gave rise to this joke: a woman became pregnant and went to Coué to ask how she could ensure that her child grew up with good manners. She was told to say many times every day: 'My Child Will Be Polite And Good-Mannered', or words to that effect. Nine months passed and no child was born. Years went by and still no child appeared. Eventually, the lady, now quite old, died and a post-mortem was held. As the body was opened, there stood two tiny old men with long white hair and beards, saying to each other: 'Après vous, m'sieur'; 'Non, non, après vous.')

Fidelity, Bravery, Integrity   The US Federal Bureau of Investigation, based on its initials F.B.I.

How To Win Friends And Influence People   More than the title of a book. Dale Carnegie's courses incorporating the principle had been aimed at business people for a quarter of a century when, in 1936, an ad campaign launched Carnegie's book on self-improvement. As a result, a million copies were sold between December 1936 and November 1939.

The Mounties Always Get Their Man Unofficial motto of the Royal Canadian Mounted Police.

My Word Is My Bond Bargains are made 'on the nod' at the London Stock Exchange, with no written pledges given or documents exchanged. Hence the motto.

Nation Shall Speak Peace Unto Nation The British Broadcasting Corporation's motto was suggested by Dr Montague Rendall, one of the first five governors, when the coat of arms was chosen in 1927. It echoes a passage in Micah 4:3: 'Nation shall not lift up a sword against nation'. In 1932, however, it was decided that the BBC's mission was not to broadcast to other nations but to provide a service for home consumption – and for the Empire. **Quaecunque** ('whatsoever') was introduced as an alternative reflecting the Latin inscription, also composed by Dr Rendall, in the entrance hall of Broadcasting House, London, and based on Philippians 4:8: 'Whatsoever things are beautiful and honest and of good report'. In 1948 'Nation Shall Speak Peace Unto Nation' came back into use as the Corporation's main motto – appropriately, after the BBC's notable role promoting international understanding during the Second World War.

Peace Is Our Profession US Strategic Air Command.

Small Is Beautiful Professor E. J. Schumacher's prescription for economics on a human scale (used as the title of his 1973 book) is clearly not a slogan because it does not promote a product or a cause within a specific organisation or framework. Therefore it is a maxim or guiding principle, although one could imagine it being used as a motto or slogan.

Who Dares, Wins UK Special Air Service regiment (SAS). (After they had shot their way into the Iranian Embassy in London in May 1980 and ended the siege there, wags suggested that the motto should be: 'Who dares use it, wins.')

MONEY, MONEY, MONEY

Access Takes The Waiting Out Of Wanting   Access credit card; UK, *c.* 1973. Withdrawn after protests about the ethics of the pitch and replaced by **Makes Sensible Buying Simple**. More recently: **Access – Your Flexible Friend** (UK, current 1981).

At The Sign Of The Black Horse   Lloyd's Bank; UK, current 1980. This slogan capitalises upon the bank's black horse symbol, which dates back to 1666.

Before You Invest – Investigate   The National Better Business Bureau Inc.; US, current 1941. Suggested by S. P. Halle, President of Halle Brothers, while a member of the Cleveland Better Business Bureau. Designed to warn prospective investors.

Come And Talk To The Listening Bank   Midland Bank; UK, from 1980. A slogan that turned sour when a twenty-year-old student was *arrested* when she went to see her manager about her overdraft.

Don't Leave Home Without It   American Express credit card; US, current 1981. In the UK in the late 1970s, **That Should Do Nicely, Sir!**, a fawning line from an Amex TV ad which became a catchphrase.

For God's Sake Care, Give Us A Pound   Created by the KMP Partnership in 1968 for the Salvation Army. David Kingsley says: 'This was a product of a team led by myself. The truth is, I put up "For God's Sake, Give Us A Pound" to the then General of the Salvation Army and he and I revised it to "For God's Sake Care . . ." for obvious reasons.'

Get The Abbey Habit   Abbey National Building Society; UK, current late 1970s.

His Hands Are Insured For Thousands, But He Suffers From Athlete's Foot/He's A Big Shot In Steel, But He's A Dental Cripple All The Same   insurance company (name unknown); US, current *c.* 1934.

Cardiff 1967. Sidney Graves. Old Soldier. No friends. No family. No money. No home. But nobody cared. Nobody. We found him too late. He died.

For God's sake care, give us a pound.

Post to. Dept. 24 Salvation Army, 101, Queen Victoria Street, LONDON, E.C.4

Photo. David Steen

The Man From The Pru Prudential Assurance Co. Ltd; UK, current from late 1940s. The firm was founded in 1848 and the phrase evolved from what people called the person who collected their life-insurance premiums. It had become a music-hall joke by the end of the century but there was no serious use of it as a slogan by the company until after the Second World War, when it appeared in ads as **Ask The Man From The Pru**.

Merrill Lynch Is Bullish About America Merrill Lynch bank; US, current 1972. Also **A Breed Apart** (current 1980) – though not quite as apart as all that: the phrase has also been used by Triumph motorcycles in the UK.

The Prudential Has The Strength Of Gibraltar Prudential Insurance Co. of America; US, from 1896. Mortimer Remington of JWT was commuting to work in New York when, crossing the New Jersey meadows, he passed Snake Rock. This made him think of Gibraltar in answer to the Prudential President's demand for some 'symbol of lasting, enduring strength'.

We're With The Woolwich Woolwich Equitable Building Society; UK, current late 1970s. In response to the question 'Are You With The Woolwich?' in TV ads. From the accompanying jingle came the phrase 'The Safe Place, With The Nice Face', and the nice face had a peculiarly ingratiating way of saying 'Good Morning'.

PARDON MY BOAST

The danger in all sloganeering is that people will remember your slogan but not the cause or product that it promotes. Nowhere is this danger greater than in the field of 'corporate apologias' – institutional advertising where, as Daniel Boorstin says in *The Image*, we are made to think of the Du Pont Corporation not as 'Merchants of Death' but as providing **Better Things For Better Living, Through Chemistry**.

In 1955, Ronald Reagan became host of the popular programme *General Electric Theater*. Each edition ended with his intoning the line: **At General Electric Progress Is Our Most Important Product**. At least, that corporate tag was closely linked to the name of the company.

Here are twenty more phrases to be matched to twenty companies. They seem, for the most part, interchangeable. Link them up and compare your answers with the correct ones. (In Britain, corporate goo is less prevalent, so only the first five slogans may be known to most readers.)

1 **Simply Years Ahead**
2 **The Pathfinders**
3 **Yours Faithfully**
4 **Home Of Good Health**
5 **Getting Bigger By Being Better**
6 **Today Something We Do Will Touch Your Life**
7 **A Powerful Part Of Your Life**
8 **Getting People Together**
9 **We Make Things That Bring People Closer**
10 **Computers Help People Help People**
11 **Ideas To Build On**
12 **Making Machines Do More, So Men Can Do More**
13 **We're Working To Keep Your Trust**
14 **A Concern For The Future**
15 **Think What We Can Do For You**
16 **We Build Your Kind Of Truck**
17 **We Guarantee Tomorrow Today**
18 **Always The Leader**
19 **Take Stock In America**
20 **A Household Name, At Work**

a	Union Carbide	k	Scott Paper
b	Boeing	l	Wander Foods
c	Texaco	m	Westinghouse
d	Johns-Manville	n	IBM
e	PPG Industries	o	Philips
f	International Harvester	p	New York Life
g	Mack Trucks	q	Amoco
h	Trust Houses Forte	r	Bank of America
i	Western Electric	s	Sperry Rand
j	US Savings Bonds	t	ICI

ANSWERS

1:o	5:q	9:i	13:c	17:p
2:t	6:a	10:n	14:e	18:g
3:h	7:m	11:d	15:r	19:j
4:l	8:b	12:s	16:f	20:k

NOW IS THE TIME FOR ALL GOOD MEN...

Just in case there is anybody under the impression that **Now Is The Time For All Good Men To Come To The Aid Of The Party** has anything to do with communism, let it be said that it is as much a slogan as **The Quick Brown Fox Jumps Over The Lazy Dog**. They are both typewriter exercises. Charles E. Weller, a court reporter, originated 'Now Is The ...' in Milwaukee in 1867 to test the efficiency of the first practical typewriter, which his friend Christopher L. Scholes had made. Unfortunately, he did not do a very good job because the phrase only contains eighteen letters of the alphabet, whereas 'The Quick Brown Fox ...' has all twenty-six. The latter was once thought to be the shortest sentence in English containing all the letters of the alphabet but it was superseded by 'Pack My Box With Five Dozen Liquor Jugs' (which has three fewer letters overall).

Workers Of The World, Unite!   The current slogan of Industrial Workers of the World is taken from the *Communist Manifesto* (1848) of Marx and Engels: 'Let the ruling classes tremble at a communist revolution. The proletarians have nothing to lose but their chains. They have a world to win. Working men of all lands, unite!'

All Power To The Soviets   Petrograd workers, November 1917.

Toilers in Agriculture! Strengthen The Fodder Basis Of Animal Husbandry! Raise The Production And Sale To The State Of Meat, Milk, Eggs, Wool And Other Products!   One of seventy-five May Day slogans prepared by the Soviet Communist Party's Central Committee in 1980.

PEACE FOR OUR TIME

In the run-up to the Second World War, the hollowest slogan of all was Neville Chamberlain's phrase **Peace For Our Time**. On 30 September 1938 he returned from signing the Munich agreement with Hitler. He hoped that his concessions (including the virtual dismemberment of Czechoslovakia) would pave the way for peace. If Hitler honoured the agreement, well and good. If he did not, then at least the world would be able to see that he was clearly guilty. And, to be fair to Chamberlain, such was the desire for peace in Europe that, whatever personal misgivings he may have had (and there is evidence that he experienced great discomfort at the role he had to play), he was swept along with the tide.

That night he spoke from a window at 10 Downing Street, 'not of design but for the purpose of dispersing the huge multitude below' (according to his biographer, Keith Feiling). He said: 'My good friends. This is the second time in our history that there has come back from Germany to Downing Street peace with honour. I believe it is peace for our time. Go home and get a nice quiet sleep.'

Two days before, however, when someone had suggested the Disraeli phrase **Peace With Honour**, Chamberlain had impatiently rejected it, as Feiling records. A week later, Chamberlain was asking the House of Commons not to read too much into words 'used in a moment of some emotion, after a long and exhausting day, after I had driven through miles of excited, enthusiastic, cheering people'.

Disraeli had been talking about the Berlin Treaty of 1878 which forced the Russians to make a number of concessions but created rather more problems than it solved. In an impromptu speech from the steps of his railway carriage at Dover on 16 July, he said: 'Gentlemen, we bring you peace; and I think I may say, peace with honour.' Later that day in London he repeated the claim: 'Lord Salisbury and myself have brought you back peace – but a peace, I hope, with honour, which may satisfy our sovereign and tend to the welfare of the country.'

Chamberlain's phrase is often misquoted as 'Peace *in* our time', as by Noel Coward in the title of a play set at the time of the Munich agreement. Perhaps he, and others, were influenced by the phrase from the *Book of Common Prayer*: 'Give Peace in our time, O Lord.'

THE PURSUIT OF HAPPINESS

Taking their cue from the title of a 1962 Peanuts book by Charles M. Schulz, *Happiness is a Warm Puppy*, sloganeers went nuts on the 'Happiness is ...' theme from the mid-1960s onwards, gradually watering down the original:

Happiness Is Egg-Shaped   (UK, selling eggs)

Happiness Is A Quick-Starting Car   (US, Esso)

Happiness Is A Cigar Called Hamlet   (UK)

Happiness Is Being Elected Team Captain – And Getting A Bulova Watch   (US)

Happiness Is A $49 Table   (US, Brancusi Furniture)

Happiness Is Giving Dad A Terry Shave Coat For Christmas   (US, Cone Sporterry)

Happiness Is The Sands   (US, Las Vegas hotel)

Happiness Is A Bathroom By Marion Wieder   (US, decorator)

Happiness Can Be The Color Of Her Hair   (US, Miss Clairol)

Happiness Is Being Single   (bumper sticker, seen in NYC, 1981)

Happiness Is Slough In My Rear-View Mirror   (car sticker, seen in London, 1981)

No wonder Lennon & McCartney wrote a song called 'Happiness is a Warm Gun'.

HAPPINESS IS A CIGAR CALLED HAMLET.

READ ALL ABOUT IT

When newspapers and magazines come to promote themselves we are generally not impressed. Even the brightest and sanest publications can be made to sound smug and off-putting. There is something about the ethos of newspapers and magazines which is incompatible with their attempts at sloganeering. How can they appear to be sensible and reasonable organs when they have to pitch for custom like soap powders?

All Human Life Is There   *News of the World*; UK, from c. 1958–9. The only reference to this phrase in the *Oxford Dictionary of Quotations* appears under Henry James. Even if we had never read his 'Madonna of the Future' (1879) – and we had not – we were told that it contained the line: 'Cats and monkeys, monkeys and cats – all human life is there.' What was the connection, if any, with the steamy British Sunday newspaper?

Maurice Smelt takes up the story: '"All Human Life Is There" was my idea, but I don't, of course, pretend that they were my words. I simply lifted them from the *Oxford Dictionary of Quotations*. I didn't bother to tell the client that they were from Henry James, suspecting that, after the Henry–James–Who–He? stage, he would come up with tiresome arguments about being too high-hat for his readership. I did check whether we were clear on copyright, which we were by a year or two. The agency I was then working for was Colman, Prentis & Varley. I do recall its use as baseline in a tiny little campaign trailing a series that earned the *News of the World* a much-publicised but toothless rebuke from the Press Council. The headline of that campaign was: "'I've Been A Naughty Girl' Says Diana Dors". The meiosis worked, as the *News of the World* knew it would. They ran an extra million copies of the first issue of the series.'

All The News That's Fit To Print   *New York Times*; US, from 1896. This slogan was devised by Adolph S. Ochs when he bought the *New York Times* and it has been published in every edition since – at first on the editorial page, on 25 October 1896, and from the following February on the front page. It became the paper's war-cry in the 1890s battle against formidable competition from the *World*,

"All the News
That's Fit to Print"

Herald, and *Journal*. It has been parodied by Howard Dietz as 'All The News That Fits We Print' and at worst sounds like a slogan for the suppression of news. However, no paper prints everything.

Forward With The People *Daily Mirror*; UK, from *c*. 1935 until 1959. This slogan appeared on the paper's mast-head, though some who thought the paper had a way of anticipating the inevitable said the slogan ought to have been 'Sideways With The People'.

Never Underestimate The Power Of A Woman *Ladies' Home Journal*; US, from *c*. 1941. Gordon Page of N. W. Ayer recalled: 'It came off the back burner of a creative range where ideas simmer while the front burners are preoccupied with meeting closing dates ... it was just a more direct way of stating the case for the leading woman's magazine of the day. But always believing that you can do things with a twinkle that you can't do with a straight face, it was trotted to Leo Lionni ... it's largely *his* fault that you can't say "never underestimate the power of *anything*," today, without echoing the line.' (Watkins). Even in 1981, the following ad was appearing in the *New York Times*: 'Ladies' Home Journalism – Never Underestimate Its Power'.

Sunday Isn't Sunday Without The Sunday Times *Sunday Times*; UK, from 1968. Peter Phillips recalls: 'In 1968 I asked the whole creative department at Thomson Group Marketing to come up with a slogan for the *Sunday Times* and the person who presented me with this deathless slogan was Frank Page, later-motoring correspondent of *The Observer*. I was not aware that the *Empire News* had already used it (as **Sunday Isn't Sunday Without The Empire News**) – nor were the countless people who have claimed authorship since then.' (*Campaign*, 17 April 1981)

Top People Take The Times *The Times*; UK, from 1957. In the mid-1950s, the London *Times* was shedding circulation, the end of post-war newsprint rationing was in sight, and an era of renewed competition in Fleet Street was about to begin. In 1954, the paper's agency, the London Press Exchange, commissioned a survey to discover people's attitudes towards 'The Thunderer'. They chiefly found it dull, but the management of *The Times* was not going to change anything, least of all allow contributors to be identified by name. *The Times* would have to be promoted for what it was. A

The New York Times

Top People...

take **THE TIMES**

pilot campaign in provincial newspapers included one ad showing a top hat and a pair of gloves with the slogan **Men Who Make Opinion Read The Times**.

It was not the London Press Exchange but an outsider who finally encapsulated that idea in a more memorable slogan. G. H. Saxon Mills was one of the old school of advertising copywriters and had been copy director at Crawford's. But he was out of a job when he bumped into Stanley Morison of *The Times*. As a favour, Mills was asked to produce a brochure for visitors to the newspaper. When finished, it contained a series of pictures of the sort of people who were supposed to read the paper – a barrister, a trade-union official, and so on. Each was supported by the phrase: 'Top People Take The Times'.

This idea was adopted for the more public promotional campaign and first appeared in poster form during 1957, running into immediate criticism for its snobbery. But sales went up and, however toe-curling it may have been, the slogan got the paper noticed and ran on into the early 1960s.

REMEMBER, REMEMBER...

Remember **********! has been a common theme of slogans, particularly enabling wars to begin or continue by keeping alive a cause of anger:

Remember The River Raisin! A war-cry of Kentucky soldiers dating from the War of 1812. In the Raisin River massacre, 700 Kentuckians, badly wounded trying to capture Detroit, were scalped and butchered by Indians who were allies of the British.

Remember The Alamo! The Alamo Mission in San Antonio, Texas, was used as a fort during the rebellion against Mexican rule in 1836. On 6 March, five days after Texas declared her independence, President Antonio López de Santa Anna with more than 3,000 men attacked the Alamo. In it were a hundred or so Texans, including Davy Crockett. After a thirteen-day siege, every Texan had been killed or wounded, and even the wounded were put to death. López was defeated and captured at the Battle of San Jacinto,

21 April 1836, by a Texan army under Commander-in-Chief Sam Houston. Sidney Sherman, a colonel in this army, is credited with devising the battle-cry. **Remember Goliad!** from the same conflict refers to Santa Anna's shooting of 330 Texans who had retreated from Goliad.

Remember The Maine!   The US battleship *Maine* exploded and sank in Havana harbour on 15 February 1898, taking 258 American lives with it. The vessel had been sent to protect US residents and their property during the Cuban revolution. The cause of the explosion was never established, but the Spanish-American War started ten weeks later. (Graffito reported shortly after: 'Remember the Maine, To hell with Spain, Don't forget to pull the chain'.)

Remember The Lusitania!   The *Lusitania* was a British liner carrying many American passengers which was sunk off the Irish coast on 7 May 1915 by a German submarine. The sinking helped bring the US into the First World War.

Remember Belgium!   Originally a recruiting slogan referring to the invasion of Belgium by the Germans at the start of the First World War. It eventually emerged with ironic emphasis amid the mud of Ypres, encouraging the rejoinder: 'As if I'm ever likely to forget the bloody place!' (Partridge)

Remember Pearl Harbor!   The initial war-slogan and battle-cry of the US after the bombing of Pearl Harbor by the Japanese in December 1941.

Remember The Pueblo!   A bumper sticker with one of the rare battle-cries of the Vietnam War. Coined by Young Americans For Freedom following the capture of the USS *Pueblo* by North Korea in 1968.

THE SHOUT HEARD ROUND THE WORLD

Coca-Cola bids fair to be the most widely advertised product in the world. It would be hard to find a country unfamiliar with the logo and the simple injunction (in whatever language) to **Drink Coca-Cola**. Dr John Pemberton invented the drink in 1886. By 1890 the company was spending $11,000 a year on advertising. The drink was first sold outside the US in 1899. Coca-Cola today spends $184 million world-wide on advertising.

Much of the emphasis has been on driving away competitors. Among them: Caro-Cola, Fig Cola, Candy Cola, Cold Cola, CayOla, Koca-Nola, Coca, Cola, Coca-Kola, Kora-Nola, Kola Nola, KoKola, Co Kola, Coke Ola, Kos Kola, Toca-Cola, Soda Cola. Hence the continuing necessity to maintain that 'Coke' is 'the real thing'. This idea appeared in 1942 as **The Only Thing Like Coca-Cola Is Coca-Cola Itself**. **It's The Real Thing** followed in 1970. Pepsi Cola is the only major rival.

Do you remember these other slogans out of the scores that have been used?

Coke Adds Life (from 1976)
Have A Coke And A Smile (current 1980)
I'd Like To Buy The World A Coke (from 1971) The jingle became a hit in its own right when retitled 'I'd Like to Teach the World to Sing'.
It's The Refreshing Thing To Do (current 1937)
The Pause That Refreshes (from 1929)
Things Go Better With Coke (from 1963)
Thirst Knows No Season (from 1922)

Pepsi Cola is now consumed in as many countries as Coca-Cola and has achieved this in a shorter time and, for many years, with considerably less expenditure on advertising. Value for money was always aimed at in the product itself:

Come Alive – You're In The Pepsi Generation US, from 1964. This slogan presented certain problems in translation. In German it came out as 'Come alive out of the grave', and in Chinese 'Pepsi brings your ancestors back from the dead'.

Makes a light lunch refreshing

Coca-Cola has the charm of purity. It is prepared with the finished art that comes from a lifetime of practice. Its delicious taste never loses the freshness of appeal that first delighted you...always bringing you a cool, clean sense of complete refreshment. Thirst asks nothing more.

COPYRIGHT 1940, THE COCA-COLA COMPANY

Your favorite soda fountain, your favorite sandwich, and America's favorite refreshment ...ice-cold Coca-Cola. Quick-as-a-wink you're refreshed and on your way. That's why you hear so many busy people at lunch saying: "and a Coca-Cola." Try it yourself.

5¢

Drink

Coca-Cola

TRADE MARK REG U S PAT OFF

Delicious and Refreshing

THE PAUSE THAT REFRESHES

Lipsmackin thirst quenchin (ace tastin motivatin good buzzin cool talkin high walkin fast livin ever givin cool fizzin) **Pepsi**   UK, from 1974. From a jingle written by John Webster at Boase Massimi Pollitt.

Twice As Much For A Nickel, Too   US, current 1930s. Walter Mack is credited with writing this 'first advertising jingle in history' (it was sung to the tune of 'John Peel'), much used on American radio in the 1930s – indeed, an estimated six million times. After the Second World War, the value-for-money principle went out of the window and the price of Pepsi had to be raised to six and then seven cents. Consequently, the jingle had to be revised to **Twice As Much And Better, Too**. (Louis)

You've Got A Lot To Live, Pepsi's Got A Lot To Give   US, current 1960s. James B. Somerall, Pepsi's President at the time of the Vietnam War, claimed that this slogan drew attention to America's 'new national pastime – living, and making every second count.'

Best By Taste Test   Royal Crown Cola; US, current 1944.

Drink Tizer, The Appetizer   Tizer; UK, current from 1920s.

Freshen-Up With 7-Up   7-Up; US, current 1962. Alternatively, **Bring On The _Real_ Thirst-Quencher!** and **The Un-Cola**.

It's In The Public Eye   Squirt; US, quoted 1958. Well, it would be, from a product called Squirt.

One Crazy Calorie   Tab; US, quoted 1980.

LEGAL, DECENT, HONEST, TRUTHFUL

That 'All advertisements should be legal, decent, honest and truthful' is one of the essences of good advertising, according to the British Code of Advertising Practice. However, if you are feeling a mite punch-drunk from the assertiveness of the slogans in this book, it may come as some balm to be told of ones that backfired because they failed to achieve their end – and left egg all over the face of those who coined them.

America Cannot Stand Pat In the 1960 presidential election, John F. Kennedy quoted **Stand Pat With KcKinley** as an example of Republican reaction. So Richard Nixon countered with 'America Cannot Stand Pat' – until it was politely pointed out that he was married to a woman with that name. **America Cannot Stand Still** was rapidly substituted.

Flat Out On Ethyl Well, you see, there was this brand of petrol in the 1920s derived from tetraethyl lead. It is no longer available.

Grieve For Lincoln A Conservative candidate's slogan. He lost.

Once You've Driven One, You're Unlikely To Drive Another Say that again? Mercedes-Benz ad, quoted 1980.

Sounds Better Than it Looks Perhaps it is as well that we do not know the name of the TV set which is advertised all over India thus.

Vote For Any Candidate, But If You Want Well-Being And Hygiene, Vote For Pulvapies The town of Picoaza in Ecuador was treated to this slogan during a local campaign for mayor in 1967. Pulvapies was not the name of a candidate but of a locally produced foot-powder. And, when it came to the ballot, 'vote for Pulvapies' was exactly what the Picoazans did.

You're Never Alone With A Strand The slogan of a, by now, classic British ad which caught the public imagination and yet failed to achieve its purpose – selling cigarettes. Devised in 1960 by John May of S. H. Benson for the W. D. & H. O. Wills tobacco

YOU'RE NEVER ALONE WITH A **STRAND**

THE CIGARETTE OF THE MOMENT

MILLEFIL TIPPED

3'2 for twenty
(1/7 for ten)

STRAND
TIPPED CIGARETTES
W.D.&H.O.WILLS

STR 9

The moment you handle the packet you know. This is a different cigarette. Flip top pack. Sleek. Smart. Modern. No loose bits in the pocket. New Strand.

The moment you touch the cigarette you know. This is a different cigarette. Rounder. Firmer. Perfectly made—perfectly packed. New Strand.

The moment you draw you know. Taste all there. So smooth. So cool. Rich Virginia tobacco and millefil tipped. New Strand.

The moment you offer them you know. They're wanted. They're expected. They're absolutely *right*. New Strand.

MADE BY W.D. & H.O. WILL

company, the campaign was to launch a new, cheap filter cigarette called Strand. Wills had rejected the first plan put to them and so, at rather short notice, John May thought up a new concept. This amounted to appealing to the youth market by associating the cigarettes not with sex or social ease but with 'the loneliness and rejection of youth'. 'The young Sinatra was the prototype of the man I had in mind,' says May. 'Loneliness had made him a millionaire. I didn't see why it shouldn't sell us some cigarettes.'

And so a Sinatra-clone was found in the shape of a 28-year-old actor called Terence Brook, who was also said to bear a resemblance to James Dean. He was shown mooching about lonely locations in raincoat and hat. In no time at all he had his own fan-club. Music from the TV ad, 'The Lonely Man Theme', became a hit in its own right.

But the ads did not work. Viewers revised the slogan in their own minds to mean: 'If you buy Strand, then you'll be alone.' However much the young may have identified with the figure in the ad they did not want to buy him or his aura. Or perhaps it was just not a very good cigarette. Either way, it has not been forgotten.

SOFT SOAP

Body Odour (or **B.O.**)   Lifebuoy soap; US, current from 1930s. A notable phrase given to the language by advertising. On US radio in the 1930s they used to sing the jingle:

Singing in the bathtub, singing for joy,
Living a life of Lifebuoy –
Can't help singing, 'cos I know
That Lifebuoy really stops B.O.

The initials 'B.O.' were sung *basso profundo*, emphasising the horror of the offence. In the UK, TV ads showed pairs of male or female friends out on a spree, intending to attract partners. When one of the pair was seen to have a problem the other whispered helpfully, 'B.O.'

Good Morning! Have You Used Pears' Soap?   UK, current 1888 (still in use 1928). Thomas J. Barratt (1842–1914) has been dubbed, with good reason, the 'father of modern advertising', in the UK at least. With remorseless energy and unflagging invention he flooded the country with ads for Pears' soap from 1875 onwards.

'Any fool can make soap,' he said. 'It takes a clever man to sell it.' Some of his work also appeared in the US. Early on, Barratt 'decided he must have a catchphrase which would make the whole country say "Pears' Soap". His staff were invited to nominate the commonest phrase in daily use. Inevitably, somebody suggested "Good morning". The result was the notorious "Good Morning! Have You Used Pears' Soap?" which scourged two continents.

There were many who never forgave Thomas Barratt for debasing this traditional, friendly greeting. The sensitive shrank from saying ''Good morning'', knowing that it would only spark off the exasperating counter-phrase in the mind of the person addressed.' (Turner)

How Do You Spell Soap? Why P-E-A-R-S, Of Course UK, current 1880s, can hardly have been a less trying catchphrase.

Cleanliness Is Next To Godliness Although this phrase appears in one of John Wesley's sermons, it is within quotation marks and without attribution. Thomas J. Barratt could hardly be expected to leave it alone. On a visit to the US in the 1880s, he sought a testimonial from a man of distinction. Shrinking from an approach to President Grant, he ensnared the eminent divine, Henry Ward Beecher. Beecher happily complied with Barratt's request and wrote a short text beginning: 'If cleanliness is next to Godliness . . .' and received no more for his pains than Barratt's 'hearty thanks'.

Two years ago I used your soap. Since when I have used no other!

He Won't Be Happy Till He Gets It UK, current 1880s (US, current 1888). Coupled with the picture of a baby stretching out of his bath to pick up a cake of Pears' soap. 'Cartoonists freely adapted this poster, converting the baby into the Czar or the Kaiser, and the cake of soap into the disputed territory of the day.' (Turner). There was also a companion picture with the slogan **He's Got It And He's Happy Now**. In early editions of *Scouting for Boys*, Robert Baden-Powell used the original slogan (with acknowledgement to Pears) to refer to the achievement of the scouts' first-class badge.

Lillie Langtry, the noted actress of the period, came near to coining the phrase **Since When I Have Used No Other** when she wrote in a testimonial: 'Since using Pears' Soap I have discarded all others.' The precise wording came from a cartoon parody drawn by Harry Furniss which appeared in *Punch*, 26 April 1884. This showed a grubby tramp penning his own testimonial with the words: 'Two years ago I used your soap since when I have used no other.' Not missing a trick, Pears, with permission from *Punch*, added the firm's name to the cartoon and issued it as one of thousands of handbills distributed in the 1880s and 1890s.

Preparing To Be A Beautiful Lady UK, from 1932 – when young girls, some with their mothers, were featured using Pears' soap. In 1981, an announcement for the 'Miss Pears Contest' was still employing the phrase: 'We're looking for a radiant little girl who is preparing to be a beautiful lady by using pure transparent Pears' Soap every day.'

Mrs. LANGTRY says—
Since using **PEARS' SOAP** for the hands and complexion I have discarded all others.
Lillie Langtry

Keep That Schoolgirl Complexion   Palmolive soap; US, from 1917. Coined by Charles S. Pearce, a Palmolive executive. Beverley Nichols wrote in *The Star-Spangled Manner* (1928) that in his 'riotous youth' he was comforted through 'numberless orgies' only by the conviction that if he used a certain soap he would retain his schoolboy complexion:

'It did not matter how much I drank or smoked, how many nameless and exquisite sins I enjoyed – they·would all be washed out in the morning by that magic soap . . . I bought it merely because years ago a bright young American sat down in an office on the other side of the Atlantic and thought of a slogan to sell soap. And he certainly sold it.'

During the Second World War, Palmolive was still plugging the old line in the UK: 'Driving through blitzes won't spoil that schoolgirl complexion'.

99 44/100 Per Cent Pure   Ivory Soap; US, from c. 1882. One of the clumsiest but most enduring slogans of all. Nobody remembers who first coined this bizarre line but it has stuck, along with the claim that **It Floats**. A story has it that the floating character of the soap was not recognised until a dealer asked for another case of 'that soap that floats'. (In 1974, a gangster film with Richard Harris was entitled *99 And 44/100 Per Cent Dead*. For the benefit of non-Americans who would not understand the allusion, the film was tardily retitled *Call Harry Crown*. *Variety* opined crisply that it was 'As clumsy as its title'.)

Portrait of a gentleman breaking a bad habit

Until the very moment of our picture the subject thereof was a confirmed user of old-fashioned sinking soaps.

He quaintly ignored the dangers lurking in the cake on the slippery tub-bottom. There was no one present to cry, "Watch your step!" You see the painfully upsetting results.

For the first time he learned the joy of lavish lather.

He noticed the lily-white cake jauntily afloat and constantly, gloriously visible in the bed-side basin.

And he went forth preaching the gospel of Ivory—permanently cured of the catch-as-catch-

IVORY SOAP

99 44/100 % Pure · It Floats

Nine Out Of Ten Screen Stars Use Lux Toilet Soap For Their Priceless Smooth Skins Lux Toilet Soap; US, from 1927. The campaign ran for twenty years and among the stars who were listed as Lux users were Fay Wray, Mary Astor, Louise Brooks, Myrna Loy, Bebe Daniels, Clara Bow and Joan Crawford.

Pearline Keeps White Things White And Bright Women Bright Pearline soap; US, current 1896.

People Who Like People Like Dial Dial soap; US, quoted 1965. Also **Aren't You Glad *You* Used Dial: Don't You Wish *Everybody* Did?** quoted 1969.

The Skin You Love To Touch Woodbury's Facial Soap; US, from 1910. The records of the Andrew Jergens Company show that 'The Skin You Love To Touch' was originally the title of a booklet about the skin and how to care for it. The *Ladies' Home Journal* for May 1911 carried it first. Carl Naether commented in *Advertising To Women* (1928): 'It is a lure to make women believe that, by using the soap in question, she will be able to cultivate a skin sufficiently beautiful to constitute an infallible safeguard against the waning of male affection. In other words, the promise was that the soap would do more for her than just cleanse her skin.'

Why Does A Woman Look Old Sooner Than A Man? Sunlight soap; UK, from *c.* 1890. William Hesketh Lever (the first Lord Leverhulme) recorded in a diary of his tour studying American publicity methods (1888) that he bought this slogan from a Philadelphia soapmaker, Frank Siddal.

You'll Look A Little Lovelier Each Day/With Fabulous Pink Camay Camay soap; UK, current *c.* 1960. One of the catchiest phrases from the early days of British commercial TV. The soap boasted **Perfume Worth 9 Guineas An Ounce** and led to a parody about a Labour politician on the BBC TV *That Was The Week That Was* show:

> You'll look a little lovelier each day
> With fabulous Douglas Jay.

You Should See Me On Sunday Knight's Family Health Soap; UK, quoted 1941.

THE EFFECT IS SHATTERING

Born 1820 – Still Going Strong   Johnnie Walker whisky; UK, from 1910. There *was* a John Walker but he was not born in 1820 – that was the year he set up a grocery, wine and spirit business in Kilmarnock. In 1908, Sir Alexander Walker decided to incorporate a portrait of his grandfather in the firm's advertising. Tom Browne, a commercial artist, was commissioned to draw the founder as he might have appeared in 1820. Lord Stevenson, a colleague of Sir Alexander's, scribbled the phrase 'Johnnie Walker, Born 1820 – Still Going Strong' alongside the artist's sketch of a striding, cheerful Regency figure. It has been in use ever since.

The Brandy Of Napoleon   Courvoisier brandy; UK, from 1909. Napoleon really did drink it. When the former French Emperor gave himself up to the British in 1815 and was sent into exile on St Helena, a supply of the best cognac from Jarnac, selected by Emmanuel Courvoisier, travelled with him. Originally it had been intended to accompany him on a projected escape to the United States. British officers who escorted Napoleon to St Helena had many opportunities to taste the exile's cognac. In this way, Courvoisier came to be known, in English, as 'The Brandy Of Napoleon'.

Don't Be Vague – Ask For Haig   Haig whisky; UK, since *c.* 1936. The origin of this slogan is to some extent shrouded in a Scotch mist because many of the John Haig & Co. archives were destroyed during the Second World War. However, the agency thought to be responsible was C. J. Lytle Ltd. An ad survives from 1933 with the wording 'Don't Be Vague, Order Haig', another from 1935 with 'Why Be Vague? Ask for Haig', and it seems that the enduring form arose in about 1936. (In 1981, a graffito in a Belfast Protestant slum declared: 'Don't Be Vague – Starve A Taig' – 'taig' being slang for a Catholic.) It has been jocularly suggested that Haig's premium brand, Dimple, which is sold as Pinch in North America, should be promoted with the slogan 'Don't Be Simple, Ask For Dimple'.

The Perfect Round—

DON'T BE VAGUE ORDER

JOHN HAIG & CO.LTD
MARKINCH
GOLD LABEL
LIQUEUR SCOTCH WHISKY

Haig

NO FINER WHISKY GOES INTO ANY BOTTLE

Emigrate To Canada Dry (For The Sake Of Your Scotch) Canada Dry tonics and mixers; UK, current 1980. An earlier version of the slogan was used in his act by the American comedian Pat Henning: 'He was a drinkin' man, my fadder. One day he's standin' onna banks of the river, wonderin' what the hell folks can do with all that water, when suddenly he sees a great sign on the other side – DRINK CANADA DRY. [Pause] So he went up there.'

For Men Of Distinction Lord Calvert custom-blended whiskey; US, current 1945. 'For years', the copy ran, 'the most expensive whiskey blended in America, Lord Calvert is intended especially for those who can afford the finest.' Marshall McLuhan wrote in *The Mechanical Bride* (1951): 'Snob appeal might seem to be the most obvious feature of this type of ad, with its submerged syllogism that since all sorts of eminent men drink this whiskey they are eminent because they drink it. Or only this kind of whiskey is suited to the palate of distinguished men, therefore a taste for it confers, or at least displays an affinity for, distinction in those who have not yet achieved greatness.'

It Never Varies   Dewar scotch whisky; UK, from 1922.

J & B Rare Can Be Found   J & B Rare Whisky; UK, current 1980. Accompanying pictures of J & B bottles secreted in mazes, tulip fields, etc.

I Thought St Tropez Was A Spanish Monk Until I Discovered Smirnoff   Smirnoff vodka; UK, from c. 1973. The common advertising technique of the 'before' and 'after' type was given memorable form in the series of Smirnoff slogans accompanying escapist visuals from 1970 to 1975. The variations included:

It Was The 8.29 Every Morning ...

Accountancy Was My Life ...

I Never Saw Further Than The Boy Next Door ...

I Was The Mainstay Of The Public Library ...

I'd Set My Sights On A Day Trip To Calais ...

I Thought The Kama Sutra Was An Indian Restaurant ... Until I Discovered Smirnoff.

The original copywriter at Young & Rubicam was John Bacon and the art director David Tree. Tree recalled how the pair of them struggled for weeks to get the right idea. One day, after a fruitless session, he was leaving for lunch when he happened to glance at a magazine pin-up adorning the wall of the office he shared with Bacon. 'If we really get stuck,' he said, 'we can always say, "I was a boring housewife in Southgate until ..."' (Southgate was where he was living at the time.) (Kleinman)

   The were objections to the 'leg-opener', inhibition-banishing promise implicit in all this. In 1975 the Advertising Standards Authority tightened up its rules on alcohol ads, laying down that 'advertisements should neither claim nor suggest that any drink can contribute towards sexual success' and that they 'should not contain any encouragement ... to over-indulgence'. This last requirement ruled out the tag-line **The Effect Is Shattering** because it might be taken as an inducement to 'get smashed'.

The Right One   Martini; UK, from 1970. In a conscious attempt to switch Martini from being a 'woman's drink' to a 'his and hers' drink, McCann-Erickson created a romantic, high-life world full of young, beautiful people engaged in skiing, speedboating, even

ballooning. Not the least ingredient was the song composed by
Chris Gunning:

Try a taste of Martini
The most beautiful drink in the world,
It's the bright one, the right one.
There's much more to the world than you guess,
And you taste it the day you say yes
To the bright taste, the right taste
Of Martini . . .

Barry Day 'admits responsibility' for the phrase 'The Right One'. When it comes to **Any Time, Any Place, Anywhere**, Day agrees that there is more than a hint of Bogart in the line: 'As a Bogart fan of some standing, with my union dues all paid up, I think I would have known if I had lifted it from one of his utterances, but I honestly can't place it.' Also, **Martini is** ...

The Wodka From Varrington   Vladivar vodka; UK, from 1972. The unlikely positioning of Greenall-Whitley's distillery in Warrington, far from Russia or Poland, gave rise to a distinctive and enjoyable series of campaigns. The original usage was coined by Len Weinreich at the Kirkwood Company.

What Is The Secret Of Schhh?   Schweppes tonic waters and mixers; UK, from c. 1963. A phrase which caught on in a really big way. It was thought up, jointly, by Royston Taylor, copywriter, and Frank Devlin, art director, at Mather & Crowther. Taylor recalls: 'Schweppes had largely been handling their own advertising, featuring Benny Hill on TV and Stephen Potter's whimsical copy in the press. The problem was, "What can we say instead of **Schweppervescence Lasts The Whole Drink Through**"? Our idea grew very much out of the spy fever that was raging at the time. The James Bond films were just beginning, *Danger Man* was on TV (indeed, we wanted Patrick Magoohan to appear in our ads, at one stage). I came up with the idea of **Tonic Water By You-Know-Who** ... – the sort of thing you might say confidentially out of the side of your mouth in a bar. Frank Devlin suggested "The Secret of Schhh ..." which accorded with the old copywriter's dream of not showing or even naming the product if it could possibly be avoided. We compromised, just using the first three letters of the brand name and half a bottle. The comedians soon picked it up. It "made" William Franklyn, who used to appear in various comic spy situations. I suppose you could say it took Schweppes advertising out of *Punch*-style whimsy and into another area of popular whimsy – substituting one form of obscurity for another!'

You Can Take A White Horse Anywhere   White Horse whisky; UK, from 1969. The campaign which featured a white horse (but which failed to communicate any product benefit to the consumer) was masterminded in its original form by Len Heath at the KMP partnership.

STICKER SNICKER

Mid-way between the official slogan and the unofficial graffito, there is the ever-growing craze for promotional phrases emblazoned on T-shirts, lapel badges, bumper stickers and hand-drawn placards. Whereas graffiti are anonymous, this form of sloganeering suggests a measure of identification with the cause by the wearer or bearer. 'I am what I wear,' he says. He is not afraid to be counted. The slogan may not be his own work – indeed, a lapel button has probably been commercially produced – but it has a jokey, amateurish, instant appeal, which may not be true of official slogans. From the many, just a handful of the ones which do not seek to provoke a smile alone but also promote a point of view:

Lousy But Loyal   London East End slogan at George V's Jubilee, 1935.

Eleanor Start Packing, The Wilkies Are Coming   US, 1940.

Madly For Adlai   Stevenson button, US, 1952.

We Don't Like Anyone Very Much   Placard during 1964 US election.

Hitler Is Alive – In The White House   button, US, 1968.

The Family That Prays Together Stays Together   poster/bumper sticker; US, current late 1960s.

My God Is Not Dead ... Sorry 'Bout Yours   Bumper sticker, US, current 1969.

Don't Blame Me, I'm From Massachussetts   Comment on snarled peace negotiations with Hanoi, December 1972. The state had voted for George McGovern in the November election. He had promised immediate peace.

Betty Ford's Husband For President   Best-selling button of the 1976 campaign, US.

Peanut Butter Is Love – Spread Some Around Today   Placard at 1976 Democratic Convention, US.

Chile Out   Wall slogan, London, *c.* 1978. (Out of what? one might ask.) Neatly mocked by another on a Martello tower near Dublin which said 'Napoleon Out'.

A Reactor Is A Safer Place Than Ted Kennedy's Car   Window sticker, US, 1979.

More Lives Were Lost At Chappaquiddick Than At Harrisburg   Ditto.

A Blonde In Every Pond

Reagan For President, Kennedy For Chauffeur

Re-Elect Carter, Free Joan Kennedy

Nobody For President   Buttons, US, 1980.

There Is Nothing Worth Dying For   Anti-draft registration placard, US, 1980.

Piss On Disco   T-shirt, UK, 1980.

If You Can Read This – Thank A Teacher   Bumper sticker, US, 1981.

Mrs Thatcher Helps Small Businesses (Get Smaller All The Time)   Window-sticker, UK, 1981.

The Sun Never Sets On The British Empire Because God Doesn't Trust The Brits In The Dark   Irish Republican placard during New York visit of Prince Charles, June 1981.

Don't Do It, Di!   Feminist badge prior to royal wedding, UK, 1981.

STOP ME AND BUY ONE

Sweets, candies, cookies or ice cream . . . whatever it takes to bridge that gap:

And All Because The Lady Loves Milk Tray   Cadbury's Milk Tray chocolates; UK, from 1968. The pay-off line to action ads showing feats of daring of a James Bond kind and leading up to the presentation of a box of the chocolates to a suitably alluring female.

Are You A Cadbury's Fruit And Nut Case? (or 'Everyone's A . . .')   Cadbury's Fruit and Nut chocolate; UK, current 1964.

Award Yourself The C.D.M.   Cadbury's Dairy Milk chocolate; UK, from 1967–77. Devised by Dennis Auton at Young & Rubicam, this campaign invited the public, through TV, posters and press ads, to nominate worthy recipients of an award. These people then had their citations published in a style parodying the royal honours lists. Recipients included 'Miss S. Pollak, Eton Villas, London NW3, "for walking in her mini-skirt within whistling distance of the building site" (nominated by Mr T. Taylor)' and Arkle, the Grand National Steeplechase winner.

Bridge That Gap With Cadbury's Snack   Cadbury's Snack; UK, current 1967.

Chocolates With The Less Fattening Centres   Maltesers; UK, current 1965.

Desperation,   Pacification,   Expectation,   Acclamation, Realization   Fry's chocolate; UK, current after the First World War. Ads featured the faces of the famous 'five boys' anticipating a bite.

Don't Forget The Fruit Gums, Mum   Rowntree's Fruit Gums; UK, from 1958 to 1961. Coined by copywriter Roger Musgrave at S. T. Garland Advertising Services. Market research showed that most fruit gums were bought by women but eaten by children. One Friday evening, Kenneth Gill, who was in charge of the campaign, gave Musgrave this information. Over the following weekend Musgrave conceived these words as part of a jingle which was used, word for word, as written. Later on, the phrase fell foul of advertising watchdogs, who were keen to save parents from nagging. So 'mum' was amended to 'chum'.

Double Your Pleasure, Double Your Fun   Wrigley's Doublemint chewing gum; US, from 1959.

Full Of Eastern Promise   Fry's Turkish Delight; UK, current late 1950s. One of the longest-running British TV ads, appealing to escapist fantasies. One of the first showed a male slave unrolling a carpet containing a woman captive before an eastern potentate. The phrase was still in use on wrappers in 1981.

The Mint with the Hole
Made by Rowntrees

Have A Break, Have A Kit-Kat   Rowntree's Kit-Kat; UK, from *c.* 1955.

Jungle Fresh   Golden Wonder salted peanuts; UK, current late 1970s.

A Mars A Day Helps You Work, Rest And Play   Mars bar; UK, from 1960. Also **Mars Are Marvellous**.

Melts In Your Mouth, Not In Your Hand   Treets; UK, quoted 1980. Also adopted for Minstrels, current 1982.

The Mint With The Hole   Life-Savers; US, current 1920. The full phrase is: **The Candy Mint With The Hole**. Also used for Rowntree's Polo mints; UK, from 1947.

Roses Grow On You   Cadbury's Roses chocolates; UK, current mid-1960s. Norman Vaughan, who presented the TV ads, recalls: 'This was shouted at me wherever I went from about 1965. The campaign only ran for two years but on personal appearances even now (1979) people still ask me, "Where are your roses?"' Maurice Drake, who was with Young & Rubicam at the time, adds: 'This was a famous line that originally went into the waste-paper basket, but was rescued a couple of hours later, just before the cleaners came in.'

Sharp's The Word For Toffee   Sharp's toffee; UK, from 1927. Sir Edward Sharp first manufactured toffee in 1880. The old firm became Trebor Sharps Ltd during the 1960s. (Trebor is 'Robert' backwards.)

Stop Me And Buy One   Wall's ice cream; UK, from 1923. The phrase is believed to have been invented by Lionel and Charles Rodd, who were on the board of T. Wall & Sons. 8,500 salesmen with the slogan on their tricycles pedalled round Britain out of a national network of 136 depots. One salesman whose brakes failed as he descended a very steep hill introduced a slight variation as he hurtled to destruction: 'If you can stop me, you can have the lot.'

Flavour Of The Month   A generic phrase aimed at persuading people to try new varieties of ice cream and not just stick to their customary choice (principally in the US). Latterly it has become an idiom for any quickly discarded fad, craze or personal relationship.

The Sweet You Can Eat Between Meals (Without Ruining Your Appetite)   Milky Way; UK, from 1960.

Too-Good-To-Hurry-Mints   Murray Mints; UK, from late 1950s. Howard 'Boogie' Barnes wrote the lyric for one of the most catchy early British TV jingles. A typical situation was an army parade ground (in cartoon):

Sergeant: Hey, that man there!
Soldier (rifle leaning against the wall): Sorry, you'll just have to wait – I'm finishing my Murray Mint, the too-good-to-hurry-mint.
Chorus of soldiers: Murray Mints, Murray Mints,
Too-good-to-hurry-mints.
Why make haste
When you can taste
The hint of mint
In Murray Mints.

A Woman Never Forgets The Man Who Remembers   Whitman's Sampler chocolates and confections; US, current 1954. Also **Give Whitman's Chocolates – It's The Thoughtful Thing To Do**, coined in 1933 to remind people that 'social graces had not been lost in the slump'. (Lambert)

Wot A Lot I Got   Smarties; UK, from *c.* 1958 to 1964. Anthony Pugh of J. Walter Thompson recalled in 1965:
'For a long time we did dotty advertising which said that everybody likes Smarties. This was palpably untrue, because only kids did ... What we discovered was that children like collecting lots of little things – so we thought of the phrase "What a lot". Then I taped my own children playing with lots of Smarties, and they said "WOTALOTIGOT" and "WOTALOTUGOT" ... Then I thought, why don't we show the people who are supposed to be eating them, let's just get ordinary kids, not television children. The sales soared.' (Pearson)
   At the end of the TV ads came the tag **Buy Some For Lulu**.

A TASTE OF HOME

Ahh Bisto!   Bisto gravy browning; UK, from 1919. The name of the product is a hidden slogan, too. When the Cerebos company first put it on the market in 1910, the product did not have a name. According to legend, the initial letters of the proposed slogan 'Browns, Seasons, Thickens In One' were rearranged to give the brand name. The Bisto Kids, drawn by Will Owen, first appeared in 1919, sniffing a wisp of gravy aroma and murmuring, 'Ahh Bisto!' This is a phrase which has endured ever since and has been parodied in numerous cartoons over the years, providing almost a pocket history of the century – 'Ah! Ribso'; 'I Smell Bristowe!'; 'Ah, Blitzo!'; 'Ah, Bizerta'; 'Ah, Crippso!'; 'Ah! Winston!'; 'Ah! Coupon free!'; and 'Arrgh!'

Alas! My Poor Brother   Bovril meat extract; UK, current 1896. Bovril came on to the market in Britain when bold, modern advertising techniques were being applied for the first time. John Lawson Johnston, a Scot who emigrated to Canada, developed a way of blending meat extract with other raw materials. The product was first sold as Johnston's Fluid Beef in 1874. In London, S. H. Benson, a Johnston employee, set up his own business as an 'advertiser's agent' with Bovril as his first client. By the end of the century he had made Bovril a household name – and launched an advertising business that kept the Bovril account until the agency folded in 1969. 'Alas! My Poor Brother' is the most famous of the early Bovril captions, appearing with W. H. Caffyn's poster of a tearful bull eyeing a jar.

The Glory Of A Man Is His Strength   dates from this time, too. Coupled with the picture of a youth in a leopard-skin wrestling with a lion, it endured on the Bovril label for more than fifty years.

The Two Infallible Powers. The Pope And Bovril is advertising chutzpah of the first order. It appeared in the late 1890s.

I Hear They Want More, spoken by one nervous bull to another in 1903, again pointed up the somewhat uncomfortable fact of where the product originated.

It *Must* Be Bovril stemmed from an endorsement by Sir Ernest Shackleton, the explorer, in 1909. 'The question of the concentrated beef supply (on expeditions) is most important – it must be Bovril.' The phrase was still in use as late as 1936.

Give Him/Her/Them Bovril   appeared in the last campaign before the outbreak of the First World War. The Bovril airship bearing 'Give Him Bovril' on one side and 'Give Her Bovril' on the other made numerous flights over London at heights of between 100 and 1,000 feet and engaged in mock battles with a biplane, anticipating the more realistic encounters to come.

Bovril Prevents That Sinking Feeling, on H. H. Harris's cheery poster of a pyjama-clad man astride a jar at sea, ushered in the

post-war years in 1920, although the slogan was born in a golfing booklet issued by Bovril in 1890 which included the commendation: 'Unquestionably Bovril ... supplies ... the nourishment which is so much needed by all players at the critical intermediate hour between breakfast and luncheon, when the *sinking feeling* engendered by an empty stomach is so distressing, and so fruitful of deteriorated play.' It is said that Bovril had intended to use this slogan earlier but withheld it because of the *Titanic* disaster. With updated illustrations the slogan endured until 1958.

Aunt Bovril Sandwiches Grandma?   One of numerous awful puns perpetrated in Bovril advertising, especially on the railways, in the 1920s and 1930s. Others included **Bovril 2.40fy You**; **Scotch Express Great Faith In Bovril**; **If You've Mr Train Don't Miss Bovril**; **Noel Feelings To Bovril**; **Isn't The Milkmaid Attractive With Bovril? To All In Tents Bovril Is As Good As A Blanket**.

America's Most Famous Dessert   Jell-O; US, current 1900.

Babies Are Our Business   Gerber Products; US, current 1954.

Beanz Meanz Heinz   Heinz baked beans; UK, current 1967. The kind of phrase that drives teachers into a frenzy because of its apparent encouragement of poor spelling. Johnny Johnson wrote the music for the jingle which went:

> A million housewives every day
> Pick up a tin of beans and say
> Beanz meanz Heinz.

'I created the line at Young & Rubicam,' says Maurice Drake. 'It was in fact written – although after much thinking – over two pints of bitter in the Victoria pub in Mornington Crescent.'

Bet You Can't Eat Just One   Lay's potato chips; US, quoted 1981.

Can *You* Tell Stork From Butter?   Stork margarine; UK, from *c.* 1956. One of the earliest slogans on British commercial TV – endlessly referred to at the popular level. Housewives in TV ads from the Lintas agency were asked to take part in comparative tests between pieces of bread spread with real butter and Stork.

C'mon Colman's, Light My Fire   Colman's mustard; UK, current 1979. A clear echo of the Jim Morrison song 'Com' on baby, light my fire' to accompany the picture of a voluptuous woman on a tiger rug who is clearly in no need of any such encouragement. Or perhaps she is the little bit on the side.

Come Home To Birds Eye Country   Birds Eye frozen vegetables, etc.; UK, current early 1960s.

Don't Say Brown – Say Hovis   Hovis bread; UK, current from mid-1930s. Originally called Smith's Patent Germ Bread and created by Richard Smith in the 1880s, Hovis takes its name from the Latin 'hominis vis' (strength of man). In the 1930s one of the firm's paper bags showed a radio announcer saying: 'Here's a rather important announcement . . . I should have said Hovis and not just "brown".' The slogan occurred in its final form from 1956 to 1964. It still reverberates: in May 1981, when a British golfer, Ken Brown, was deserted by his caddie during a Martini championship, a *Sunday Mirror* headline was: 'Don't Say Brown, Say Novice'.

Do You Know Uneeda Biscuit?   Uneeda soda crackers; US, from 1898.

Eat More Fruit   British Fruit Trades Federation; UK, from 1923. The Federation launched a well mounted broadside 'stressing the enjoyment and good health to be derived from eating fruit. Fortuitously, an influenza epidemic broke out, enabling the promoters to point out how fruit fortified the human frame against illness.' (Turner). The campaign was a great success and paved the way for rival 'Eat More' and 'Drink More' campaigns.

The reverse form of this kind of approach was contained in the First World War slogan **Eat Less Bread**. A poster of about 1917 explained: 'The sinking of foodships by German submarines and the partial failure of the World's wheat crop have brought about a scarcity of wheat and flour which makes it imperative that every household should at once reduce its consumption of BREAD. The Food Controller asks that the weekly consumption of Bread throughout the Country should be reduced by an average of 4 lbs. per head.'

Eventually – Why Not Now?   Gold Medal Flour; US, from c. 1907. The story has it that when Benjamin S. Bull, advertising manager of the Washburn Crosby company, requested members of his department to suggest catchphrases to be used in support of Gold Medal Flour, nobody came up with anything worthwhile. Mr Bull demanded: 'When are you going to give me a decent slogan?' His underlings staved him off by saying, 'Eventually.' 'Eventually!' thundered Mr Bull, 'Why not now?'

Here's a rather important correction . . .

I should have said

HōVIS

and not just 'brown'

little jack horner wrote in the corner

don't say brown – say

Hovis

Fresh To The Last Slice   Sunblest bread; UK, current early 1960s. Compare the famous Maxwell House slogan.

Glaxo Builds Bonny Babies   Glaxo (dried, skimmed milk); UK, from 1913. The slogan 'swept the country', prompting the music-hall quip about the young husband who asked: 'Who takes it – me or the wife?'

Go To Work On An Egg   British Egg Marketing Board; UK, from 1957. Fay Weldon, now known as a novelist and TV playwright, was a copywriter on the 'egg' account at Mather & Crowther. She has taken the trouble to put the record straight over her involvement in creating one of the more memorable British slogans:
   'I was certainly in charge of copy at the time "Go To Work On An Egg" was first used as a slogan as the main theme for an advertising campaign. The phrase itself had been in existence for some time and hung about in the middle of paragraphs and was sometimes promoted to base lines. Who invented it, it would be hard to say. It is perfectly possible, indeed probable, that I put those particular six words together in that particular order but I would not swear to it. Mary Gowing, a very creative and talented advertising copywriter, was in charge of the account before I took over. She died, suddenly, when I was working under her and I, as the phrase goes, stepped over the cook; that is, I took over because there was nobody else to do it. If she wrote "Go To Work On An Egg" I don't want to claim it, but I can't be sure. I certainly devised, along with the art director, Ruth Gill, **Happiness Is Egg Shaped** and **You Can Rely On The Lion** but I think **There Is A Lion On My Egg** was Mary Gowing's.' (The lion device was stamped on eggs as a kind of hallmark, but after all this effort, campaigns on behalf of eggs went out of favour.)

Graded Grains Make Finer Flour   Homepride flour; UK, current 1969. The tag-line of a series of popular TV ads featuring the Homepride flour graders, a likeable race of bowler-hatted men.

The Ham What Am   Armour & Co. meat products; US, current 1917. Accompanied by the logo of a negro chef – suggested by a lithographer. Latterly used as a trademark for all the company's meat products, not just the ham.

Heinz 57 Varieties   Heinz canned foods; US, from 1896. In that year Henry Heinz was travelling through New York City on the overhead railway. He saw a streetcar window advertising 21 styles of shoe, the idea appealed to him and, although he could list about 58 or 59 Heinz products, he settled on 57 because it sounded right. Heinz commented later: 'I myself did not realise how successful a slogan it was going to be.' In fact, it is now as much a brand name as a slogan. (In housey-housey or bingo, 'all the beans' is now the cry for '57'.)

Go to work on an egg

It's Fingerlickn' Good Kentucky Fried Chicken; US, current 1975. Also **Real Goodness From Kentucky Fried Chicken** and **Corn And Cluck For A Buck**.

It's Not Fancy, But It's Good Horn & Hardart (restaurants using vending machines); US, current 1966.

It Takes A Tough Man To Make A Tender Chicken Perdue Farms chicken; US, current 1976. The ads featured Mr Perdue himself.

It Takes Two Hands To Hold A Whopper Whopper (hamburger); US, quoted 1981.

The Kind Mother Used To Make   New England Mincemeat; US, current 1900. One of numerous advertising lines playing on assumptions about the goodness of home produce and the good old days (reminding one of the small ad said to have made the pitch: 'Buckwheat cakes like mother used to make $1.25. Like mother thought she made $2.25.') (The title of this section also plays upon the same theme. It was devised by Barry Day as an all-purpose food slogan – but has not, to my knowledge, actually been used.)

Makes You Feel Like A Queen   Summer County margarine; UK, current 1960s.

Mr Kipling Does Make Exceedingly Good Cakes   Mr Kipling Cakes; UK, current from early 1970s.

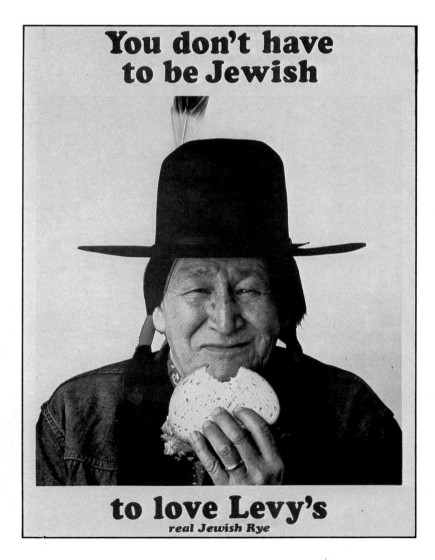

Nobody Does It Like McDonald's Can   McDonald's hamburger restaurants; US, current 1970s.

The Only 'Sauce' I Dare Give Father   Burma sauce; UK, current in the early twentieth century.

Out Of The Strong Came Forth Sweetness   Lyle's Golden Syrup; UK, current 1930s onwards. A quotation from the Book of Judges 14:14: 'Out of the eater came forth meat, and out of the strong came forth sweetness' – Samson's riddle. More recently the Tate & Lyle company has completely reversed the phrase by saying **Out Of Sweetness Came Forth Strength** as part of its occasionally necessary campaigns featuring 'Mr Cube' to ward off nationalisation of the British sugar industry.

Oxo Gives A Meal Man-Appeal   Oxo beef extract, for cooking and drinks; UK, from 1958. The Oxo cube first appeared in 1910 and has been supported by numerous slogans over the years. In the late 1950s, the Oxo company wanted TV to 'take it off the streets and put it in the home'. Copywriter Joan Drummond was told to come up with a husband-and-wife domestic situation which would dramatise the youthful image J. Walter Thompson wished to project. 'We want the idea that the chap is after the girl for her sexiness as well as her good cooking,' she was told, 'and we need a slogan to keep us on that line.' 'Oxo Gives A Meal Man-Appeal' was what she came up with. (Pearson)

See How It Runs   Cerebos salt; UK, from 1919. Cerebos salt was invented in 1894 by George Weddell, who discovered that his compound flowed much better than ordinary table salt. This property was emphasised when in 1906 the Cerebos company bought up a rival, Birdcatcher salt, whose trademark was a little boy pouring salt on a chicken's tail. He first appeared on the Cerebos packs after the First World War.

Spreads Straight From The Fridge   Blue Band margarine; UK, current late 1960s.

Sweet As The Moment When The Pod Went 'Pop'   Birds Eye peas; UK, from *c.* 1956. Written by Len Heath at the Lintas agency.

Try Our Rivals, Too   Van Camp's pork and beans; US, current in the late nineteenth century. Claude C. Hopkins said: 'I urged people to buy the brands suggested and compare them with Van Camp's ... if we were certain enough of our advantage to invite such comparisons, people were certain enough to buy.' (He had found that the executives of the company could not tell their own product and its competitors apart.)

When It Rains, It Pours Morton salt; US, from 1911. This phrase could apply to other products, but with the logo of a girl in the rain, sheltering the salt under her umbrella, it capitalised on the fact that the Morton grade ran freely from salt cellars even when the atmosphere was damp. In a small booklet describing the product a copywriter used the phrase as a paragraph heading and the slogan developed from there.

Where's George? – He's Gone To Lyonch Lyons Corner Houses; UK, current 1936. W. Buchanan-Taylor, advertising chief at Lyons, recalled: 'I resorted to the unforgivable and invented "Lyonch" as a descriptive of lunch at Lyons ... then I heard a story within the office of how a man on the advertising staff of *The Times* called one day a little later than was his wont to pick up his pal, George Warner, the head of my studio. He was so much later than usual that when he looked into the room and asked "Where's George?" the artist replied, without looking up from his work, "Gone to Lyonch, you fool." I made a note on my desk pad ... and I sent one of the staff to Somerset House to tot up the number of registered Georges in the country.' When the count had reached more than a million, the slogan was adopted. It had to be carefully obliterated during the funeral of King George V in 1936.

With A Name Like Smuckers It Has To Be Good Smucker's preserves; US, from *c.* 1960. Lois Wyse of Wyse Advertising, New York, recalls: 'Slogans come and go but "With A Name Like ..." has become a part of the language. I wrote it for a company with an unusual name in answer to a challenge from Marc Wyse who said that he didn't feel our Smucker advertising differed from the competition. The real job, however, was not thinking up the slogan but selling it to Paul Smucker. The then sales manager said: "If you run that line, Paul, we'll be out of business in six months"! But it's still in use after twenty years.'

You Don't Have To Be Jewish To Love Levy's Real Jewish Rye Levy's rye bread; US, current 1967. The point of this slogan was reinforced memorably by its being positioned under pictures of very obviously un-Jewish people – Indians, Frenchmen, or whoever. Nobody had heard of the brand until Doyle, Dane, Bernbach got to work on it. The phrase has a well established feel to it and may have been a Jewish saying before its ad use. Leo Rosten in *The Joys of Yiddish* (1968) says, 'You don't have to be Jewish to be a *folks-mensch*' – though perhaps he was influenced by the current slogan. In the UK, it ended up as the title of a radio programme for (mostly) Jews on BBC Radio London (from 1971). (Graffiti additions have been plentiful. They include: '... to be offended by this ad'/'... to be called one'/'... to go to Columbia University, but it helps'/'... to wear levis'/'... to be circumcised'.)

GOOD TO THE LAST DROP

Chock Full O'Nuts Is That Heavenly Coffee Chock Full O'Nuts coffee; US, current 1950s. Included in a jingle by Shirley Polykoff.

Good To The Last Drop Maxwell House coffee; US, from 1907. President Theodore Roosevelt was visiting Joel Cheek, perfector of the Maxwell House blend. After the President had had a cup, he said of it that it was 'Good . . . to the last drop'. It has been used as a slogan ever since, despite the various smart-alecs who have inquired 'What's wrong with the last drop then?' Professors of English have been called in to consider the problem and have ruled that 'to' can be inclusive and not just mean 'up to but not including'.

Grateful And Comforting Like Epps's Cocoa Epps's cocoa; UK, from c. 1900. In Noel Coward's play *Peace In Our Time* (1947), one character says: 'One quick brandy, like Epps's Cocoa, would be both grateful and comforting.' When asked 'Who is Epps?' he replies: 'Epps's Cocoa – it's an advertisement I remember when I was a little boy.' Also, **The Food For Strong and Weak**.

Horlicks Guards Against Night Starvation Horlicks milk drink; UK, from 1930. J. Walter Thompson evolved the concept of 'night starvation' (to add to the worries of the twentieth century – nobody had been aware of it before): 'Right through the night you've been burning up reserves of energy without food to replace it. Breathing alone takes twenty thousand muscular efforts every night.' Eric Partridge records that the phrase became a popular term for sexual deprivation. Before this, there had been the memorable picture ad of a man turning out his suitcase with the phrase **I Know I Packed It**. During the 1950s, JWT ran comic-strip sagas of the refreshing qualities of Horlicks for tired housewives, run-down executives, etc., which customarily ended with the slogan: **Thinks . . . Thanks To Horlicks**.

Hot Chocolate, Drinking Chocolate – The Late, Late Drink Cadbury's Drinking Chocolate; UK, current 1960s.

Join The Tea-Set   Typhoo tea; UK, current 1970s.

Ready, Aye, Ready   Camp coffee; UK, from *c*. 1883. This is almost a slogan in the old sense of a war-cry. It was used as such by several Scots clans, including the Johnstons, Stewarts, Napiers and Scotts. Various institutions used it as a motto, too – Merchiston Castle School, Edinburgh, is one. But it has travelled farthest on the distinctive label for Camp coffee, manufactured by R. Paterson & Sons of Glasgow. The label was virtually unchanged for nearly a hundred years. Today the basic elements still remain: a Scots officer being served coffee by a turbanned attendant with the slogan up a flagpole. Additional phrases have adjured: **Drink Camp – It's The Best!** and **Don't Be Misled!!!**

Salada Is Delicious Tea   Salada tea; US, from *c*. 1890.

Sleep Sweeter, Bournvita   Bournvita night drink, UK, current 1960s. Featured memorably in a TV commercial which simply consisted of a smiling mug and the slogan followed by a yawn and 'Goodnight'.

Spend Wisely – Save Wisely   Brooke Bond Dividend tea; UK, current 1930s.

The Tea You Can Really Taste   Brooke Bond P. G. Tips; UK, current 1960s. Also **Tea You Can Taste To The Last Delicious Drop**.

Tetley Make Tea-bags Make Tea   Tetley's tea; UK, current 1970s.

Typhoo Puts The 'T' In Britain   Typhoo tea; UK, current 1970s.

We Are The Ovaltineys/Happy Girls And Boys   Ovaltine milk drink; UK, from 1935. From one of the most evocative jingles of all. The Ovaltiney Club was launched over Radio Luxembourg. Children were given badges, rule books, secret codes and comics, and by 1939 there were five million active members. In 1946 the show was revived to run for several more years.

UP IN SMOKE

Ah, Woodbine – A *Great* Little Cigarette   Woodbine cigarettes; UK, current 1957 – using Norman Hackforth's voice-over.

...Anyhow Have A Winfield   Winfield cigarettes; Australia, current 1975. From long-running TV campaigns featuring Paul Hogan came the distinctive pronunciation of 'anyhow' as 'ennyeeiaouww..!'

The Best Tobacco Money Can Buy   Rothman's cigarettes; UK, current 1981. With equal modesty: **The Greatest Name In Cigarettes** and **The World's Most Popular King Size Filter Cigarette**.

Blow Some My Way   Chesterfield cigarettes; US, from 1926. Used – some said suggestively – when a woman made her first appearance in US cigarette advertising. **I'll Tell The World – They Satisfy** was current the same year.

Call For Philip Morris   Philip Morris cigarettes; US, current 1941. The jingle went: 'You get all the flavour and you get it mild/When you call for Philip Morris cigarettes.'

Come To Where The Flavor Is. Come To Marlboro Country   Marlboro cigarettes; US, current from mid-1950s. Originally devised by the Leo Burnett agency in Chicago as a means of shifting the appeal of Marlboro from women to men by showing it in use by rugged cowboy types. Hence **Man-Sized Flavour** but, hedging the bet, **A Man's Cigarette That Women Like Too**.

Cool As A Mountain Stream   Consulate cigarettes; UK, current early 1960s. Also **Menthol-Fresh, Cool, Clean, Consulate** (changed following the 1963 cancer scare to: **Cool, Fresh, Consulate**).

For Your Throat's Sake, Smoke Craven "A" – They Never Vary   Craven "A" cigarettes; UK, current 1920s and 1930s. A quite unbelievable line nowadays, but at the time there were others, too: **Smoke Craven "A" – Will Not Affect Your Throat** and **Craven "A" – It's Kind To Your Throat**.

I'd Walk A Mile For A Camel   Camel cigarettes; US, current early twentieth century. One day a sign-painter was painting a billboard – according to the story – when a man came up and asked him if he had a cigarette. The painter gave him a Camel. The stranger thanked him and uttered the immortal words: 'I'd walk a mile for a camel.' The painter passed the line on and from this incident came one of the best ever cigarette slogans. It was dropped in 1944.

Internationally Acknowledged To Be The Finest Cigarette In The World   Dunhill cigarettes; UK, quoted 1981.

The International Passport To Smoking Pleasure   Peter Stuyvesant cigarettes; UK, current from 1960s. Do you remember the line from the cinema ads: 'In City After City, Country After Country, More And More People Are Turning To . . .'? Also **So Much More To Enjoy**.

It's That Condor Moment   Condor pipe tobacco; UK, current 1970s.

It's Toasted   Lucky Strike cigarettes; US, current from late 1920s. Sometimes **They're Toasted** – as indeed are all cigarettes, but Lucky Strike seized the pitch. From the same period comes the line **Reach For A Lucky Instead Of A Sweet**. George Washington Hill of the American Tobacco Company was driving through New York City one day when he grabbed his colleague Vincent Riggio and cried, 'I've got it!' He had noticed a stout woman waiting to cross the street, eating a big piece of candy. Alongside, a taxi pulled up in which a 'nice-looking' woman was smoking a cigarette. The contrast precipitated this slogan. Understandably, the confectionery industry was not very pleased but it is said that this campaign created more women smokers than any other promotion. Also **No Throat Irritation – No Cough**; the 1940s radio catchphrase **LS/MFT** (Lucky Strike Means Finer Tobacco); and **So Round, So Firm, So Fully Packed** (quoted 1958).

Not A Cough In A Carload   Old Gold cigarettes; US, current 1928.

People Are Changing To Guards   Guards cigarettes; UK, current 1960s.

Player's Please   John Player & Sons cigarettes; UK, from 1927. Three years earlier this enduring slogan appeared in the form 'Player's Will Please You'. By 1925 this had become 'They're Player's And They Please'. George Green, the firm's advertising manager entered a tobacconist's shop and overheard a customer asking for 'Player's, please'. He went back to his office, wrote the phrase out in his own immaculate hand (the one used in the ads) and the slogan took on its final form. **It's The Tobacco That Counts**

was current in 1927, too. **People Love Player's** – 'a classic campaign revealing the romantic promise implicit in a puff of smoke' – was launched in 1960.

Pure Gold   Benson & Hedges cigarettes; UK, current 1964. Originally this campaign used the phrase (to reflect the gold packs) with lines like 'What's too precious to leave lying round?' Later the brand took to providing visual images that would inevitably recall the slogan, without actually using it.

Senior Service Satisfy   Senior Service cigarettes; UK, current 1981. Before 1950, there was the bizarre line **A Product Of The Mastermind**.

Winston Tastes Good Like A Cigarette Should   Winston cigarettes; US, current 1976. The slogan dealt a blow to standard usage ('as a cigarette should . . .').

You've Come A Long Way Baby (To Get Where You Got To Today)   Virginia Slims cigarettes; US, from 1968. A slogan that reflected the feminist mood of the time – indeed, the phrase has been used on Women's Lib posters.

And something to light up with:

Flick Your Bic   Bic lighters; US, from 1975. Coined by Charlie Moss, the original usage occurred in an ad that showed how smart, sophisticated people did not use lighters – they simply 'flicked their Bics'. The line became a household word in the US and was picked up by many comedians. During the energy crisis, Bob Hope said: 'Things are getting so bad that the Statue of Liberty doesn't light up any more. She just stands there and flicks her Bic.'

Smokers Are Requested To Use Swan Vestas   matches; UK, current 1920s and 1930s. The captions on the matchboxes themselves have changed to reflect current conditions: **The Smoker's Match** (1905); **Use Matches Sparingly** (1941).

Not forgetting, in the UK from 1971, on all cigarette advertising and packs:
DANGER: H.M. GOVERNMENT HEALTH DEPARTMENT'S WARNING: CIGARETTES CAN SERIOUSLY DAMAGE YOUR HEALTH.   The 'seriously' was added in 1977, the 'Danger' in 1980. David Simpson, Director of ASH (Action on Smoking and Health), comments:
'There is no law that the words should be on the packs but it is one provision of the "voluntary" agreement which the tobacco industry has entered into with the Department of Health as a preference to the possibility of legislation. For a product which will kill one in four of those who smoke twenty a day all their lives, the warnings are hopelessly inadequate.'

And in the USA:
WARNING: THE SURGEON-GENERAL HAS DETERMINED THAT CIGARETTE SMOKING IS DANGEROUS TO YOUR HEALTH.

Also, just in case that failed to scare you:

Kiss A Non-Smoker ... Enjoy The Difference!

Your Money *And* Your Life!

You Can't Scrub Your Lungs Clean

Cancer Cures Smoking
all current in the UK in 1981.

THE WAR TO END WARS

"YOUR COUNTRY NEEDS YOU"

'I launched the phrase **The War To End Wars** and that was not the least of my crimes,' confessed H. G. Wells long after the First World War was over. (*The War That Will End War* was the title of a book he had written in 1914.)

Most of the slogans that came out of the war, however, are related to recruitment:

'Alf A Mo, Kaiser! became a catchphrase after a recruiting poster had shown a British 'Tommy' lighting a cigarette prior to going into action. (The phrase even surfaced again in the Second World War as ''Alf A Mo, Hitler!')

Berlin By Christmas Initially, it was thought that the war would not last very long. (In 1939, the phrase 'All Over By Christmas' was used by some optimists as it had been in several previous wars – none of which was over by Christmas.)

Business As Usual H. E. Morgan (later Sir Herbert Morgan) was an advertising man working for W. H. Smith & Sons, who promoted this slogan which had quite a vogue until it was proved to be manifestly untrue and hopelessly inappropriate. Morgan was an advertising consultant to H. Gordon Selfridge, who consequently also became associated with the slogan. On 26 August 1914, Selfridge said: ''Business As Usual'' must be the order of the day.' In a Guildhall speech on 9 November, Winston Churchill said: 'The maxim of the British people is ''Business as usual''.'

Daddy, What Did *You* Do In The Great War? (accompanied by the picture of an understandably appalled family man puzzling over what to reply to the daughter on his knee) This recruiting slogan became a catchphrase in the form 'What did you do in the Great War, Daddy?' and gave rise to such responses as 'Shut up, you little bastard. Get the Bluebell and go and clean my medals.' (Partridge)

England Expects That Every Man Will Do His Duty And Join The Army Today An obvious extension of Lord Nelson's message to the British fleet before the Battle of Trafalgar in 1805. The original form of *that* slogan was 'Nelson Confides That Every Man Will Do His Duty' but it was suggested to him that it would be better to substitute 'England' for 'Nelson'. The signals officer, one Lieutenant Pasco, also pointed out that if 'expects' was substituted for 'confides' he need only run up one flag instead of seven (as 'expects' was a common enough word to be represented by one flag in the signals book).

Enlist Today (or rather **To-Day** as it was usually put) A key phrase in almost all recruitment copy from this war.

A Land Fit For Heroes (sometimes **A Country Fit For Heroes**) When the war was over, Lloyd George gave rise to this slogan in a speech at Wolverhampton on 24 November 1918, the exact words of which are: 'What is our task? To make Britain a fit country for heroes to live in.'

Who's Absent? Is It You? (plus a picture of John Bull)

Women Of Britain Say – *'GO!'*

Your Country Needs You The most famous recruiting slogan of all. It was used to accompany a picture of Field-Marshal Lord Kitchener, with staring eyes and pointing finger. Kitchener was appointed Secretary of State for War on 6 August 1914, two days after the outbreak. He set to work immediately, intent on raising the 'New Armies' required to supplement the small standing army of the day, which he rightly saw would be inadequate for a major conflict.

In fact, work on advertising for recruits had started the year before, with some success. Then, towards the end of July 1914, Eric Field of the tiny Caxton Advertising Agency (owned by Sir Hedley Le Bas) received a call from a Colonel Strachey, who 'swore me to secrecy, told me that war was imminent and that the moment it broke out we should have to start advertising at once'. That night, Field wrote an advertisement headed **Your King And Country Need You** with the royal coat of arms as the only illustration. The day after war was declared, 5 August, this appeared prominently in the *Daily Mail* and other papers.

Still going strong in 1981 . . .

The appeal appeared in various forms but Kitchener preferred this first slogan and insisted on finishing every advertisement with 'God Save The King'. The drawing was by the humorous artist Alfred Leete and it was taken up the same month by the Parliamentary Recruiting Committee for poster use. The original is in the Imperial War Museum. (Margot Asquith commented: 'If Kitchener was not a great man, he was, at least, a great poster.')

The idea was widely imitated abroad. In the US, James Montgomery Flagg's poster of a pointing Uncle Sam bore the legend **I Want *You* For The US Army**. (There was also a version by Howard Chandler Christy featuring a woman with a mildly come-hither look saying, **I Want You For The Navy**.)

TODAY PEORIA, TOMORROW THE WORLD

Slogans help keep the wheels of democracy churning, not only in presidential election years. Here are political cries from all over the political spectrum during two centuries and more of American history:

No Taxation Without Representation was current in the years before the War of Independence, or in the form **Taxation Without Representation Is Tyranny**, attributed to the lawyer and statesman James Otis in 1763. He opposed British taxation on the grounds that the colonies were not represented in the House of Commons. (Echoed many years later by Arnold Toynbee: 'No annihilation without representation.')

Liberty And Property, And No Stamps The motto of various American newspapers following the Stamp Act of 1765, which was the first direct tax levied upon the American colonies by the British Parliament.

United We Stand, Divided We Fall Jonathan Dickinson wrote 'The Patriot's Appeal' in 1768:

Then join hand in hand, brave Americans all!
By uniting we stand, by dividing we fall.

The State of Kentucky gave it the precise form in its 1792 motto. The idea can, however, be traced back to 550 BC and Aesop's Fable of the Four Oxen and the Lion.

Vote As You Shot Used by veterans' groups for many years after the Civil War.

Speak Softly And Carry A Big Stick Speaking at the Minnesota State Fair in September 1901, President Theodore Roosevelt gave strength to the idea of backing negotiations with threats of military force when he said: 'There is a homely adage which runs, "Speak softly and carry a big stick; you will go far." If the American nation will speak softly and yet build and keep at a pitch of the highest training a thoroughly efficient navy, the Monroe Doctrine will go

Poor Kid!
ROOSEVELT : "Well, are you going to adopt him?"

far.' The homely adage is said to have started life as a West African proverb.

Share The Wealth and **Everyman A King (But No Man Wears A Crown)** Slogans of Louisiana Governor Huey P. Long from 1928 to his assassination in 1935. The thrust of his campaign was that 10 per cent of the people owned 70 per cent of the wealth and that this should be shared. The second of the slogans is a quotation from William Jennings Bryan's 'Cross of Gold Speech' to the 1896 Democratic Convention.

The Buck Stops Here President Truman had a sign on his desk bearing these words, indicating that the Oval Office was where the passing of the buck had to cease. The phrase seems to be of his own making. When President Nixon published his memoirs, people opposed to its sale went around with buttons saying: 'The book stops here.'

Had Enough? A Republican slogan aimed at President Truman during the 1946 mid-term elections when things were going badly for him.

Over The Hump With Humphrey A sign on Hubert Humphrey's campaign bus when he sought the Democratic nomination, in vain, in 1960.

More With Gore Gore Vidal's slogan during his unsuccessful campaign as Democratic candidate for Congress in a New York district. (Unhappily, 'Vidal So Soon' appears to have been considered and rejected.)

You'll Be Safe In The Park/Every Night After Dark/With Lefkowitz, Gilhooley And Fino A dotty local election ditty from New York in 1961. There was even a version in Spanish for the Puerto Ricans (who otherwise appeared unrepresented on this cosmopolitan ticket).

Your Home Is Your Castle – Protect It   A 'code-word' slogan, designed to appeal to white voters concerned that property values would decline if blacks moved in. Used by various candidates in mayoralty and state elections. Lester Maddox won a narrow victory in the contest for the 1966 Georgia governorship with it.

Gordon Liddy Doesn't Bail Them Out, He Puts Them In   Lawyer G. Gordon Liddy (later the mastermind behind Watergate) contested a Republican congressional nomination in 1968 with this slogan and lost narrowly.

He Is Fresh When Everyone Is Tired   A John Lindsay campaign slogan from his years as Mayor of New York, giving rise to the graffiti emendation: 'He is fresh when everyone is polite.'

Would You Buy A Used Car From This Man?   A devastating slur which has attached itself permanently to the personality of Richard M. Nixon. It was recalled in poster form during the 1968 election. But how did it begin? Was it a folk saying originally? Or did a Mort Sahl or a Lenny Bruce coin it? Even my hairdresser doesn't know for sure. Compare the phrase applied to Governor George Romney: 'Would you buy a *new* car from this man?'

Give The Presidency Back To The People   Eugene McCarthy's cry, seeking the Democratic nomination in 1968 – without success.

Winning In Politics Isn't Everything, It's The Only Thing   Slogan of the Committee to Re-Elect The President in 1972. Look where it got them.

Impeach Nixon   Common cry in 1974.

Nobody Drowned At Watergate   In the early days of Watergate Nixon supporters made this pointed reference to the stonewalling by Senator Edward Kennedy after the Chappaquiddick incident.

Dog Litter – An Issue You Can't Sidestep   Corny, but a candidate for local office in Washington won with it.

WE EXCHANGED MANY FRANK WORDS IN OUR RESPECTIVE LANGUAGES

A foreign language slogan occasionally impinges upon English speech. What causes did the following phrases promote? What do they mean? The answers are on page 154 .

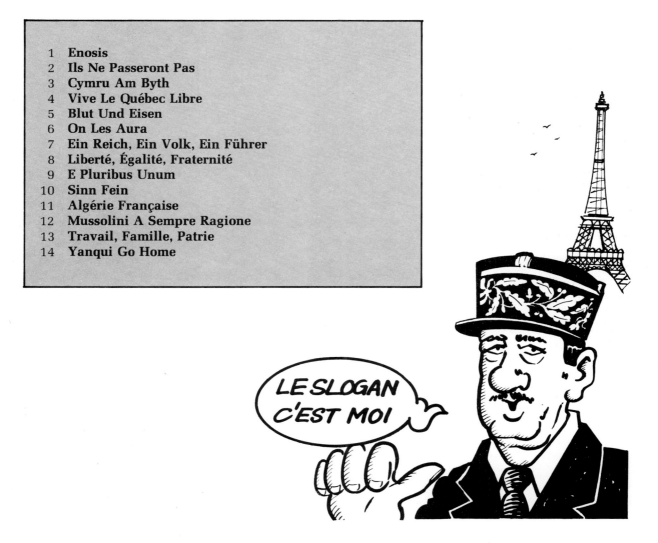

1   **Enosis**
2   **Ils Ne Passeront Pas**
3   **Cymru Am Byth**
4   **Vive Le Québec Libre**
5   **Blut Und Eisen**
6   **On Les Aura**
7   **Ein Reich, Ein Volk, Ein Führer**
8   **Liberté, Égalité, Fraternité**
9   **E Pluribus Unum**
10 **Sinn Fein**
11 **Algérie Française**
12 **Mussolini A Sempre Ragione**
13 **Travail, Famille, Patrie**
14 **Yanqui Go Home**

LE SLOGAN C'EST MOI

ANSWERS

1 ('One')   Modern Greek slogan referring to the proposed union of Cyprus with mainland Greece, from about 1952.

2 ('They Shall Not Pass')   First said to have been uttered by Marshal Pétain at Verdun, 26 February 1916. The official record appears in General Nivelle's Order of the Day (23 June 1916) as: 'Vous ne les laisserez pas passer!' The inscription on the Verdun medal is 'On ne passe pas'. Subsequently, as 'No pasarán', the phrase was used at the end of a radio speech by Dolores Ibarrurí (La Pasionara), 18 July 1936, calling on the women of Spain to help defend the Republic. It became a Republican watchword in the Spanish Civil War. (Bartlett)

3 ('Wales For Ever')   The motto of the Welsh Guards (and everybody else in the principality).

4 ('Long Live Free Quebec!')   'Extempore remarks' made by French President Charles de Gaulle during a visit to Montreal, 25 July 1967, led to his rapid departure for home, having incurred the displeasure of the Federal Government for interfering in Canada's internal affairs.

5 ('Blood And Iron')   'It is desirable and it is necessary that the conditions of affairs in Germany and of her constitutional relations should be improved; but this cannot be accomplished by speeches and resolutions of a majority, but only by iron and blood' (i.e. 'Eisen und Blut' in the original) – Bismarck, in a speech to the Budget Commission of the Prussian House of Delegates, 30 September 1862. (The Roman orator Quintilian first used the phrase 'sanguinem et ferrum' ('blood and iron') in the first century AD.)

6 ('Let 'Em Have It')   From a French poster of the First World War seeking war loans (revived in the Second World War).

7 ('One Realm, One People, One Leader')   Nazi slogan, first used at the Nuremberg Rally, September 1934.

8 ('Liberty, Equality, Fraternity')   Of earlier origin than the French Revolution, it was adopted by the revolutionary Club des Cordeliers as its offical motto on 30 June 1793. At first, the words '**Ou la mort**' ('or death') were added but were dropped from 1795.

9 ('One out of many') A line from Virgil's *Moretum* was chosen by Benjamin Franklin, Thomas Jefferson and John Adams as the US motto in 1776. It appears on the Great Seal of the United States and on all coins and banknotes, although 'In God We Trust' was formally adopted by Congress as the country's motto in 1956.

10 ('Ourselves Alone' or 'We Alone') The motto of the Irish Nationalist Movement, Sinn Fein, since about 1907. (Also adopted by Breton separatists.)

11 ('Algeria is French') Slogan of right-wing opponents of President de Gaulle, from May 1958. The rhythm of the slogan was tooted on car horns and the actual phrase often delivered as part of the longer chant, 'Vive l'Algérie Française, Vive la République, Vive la France!'

12 ('Mussolini Is Always Right') Italian fascist slogan, 1936.

13 ('Work, Family, Fatherland') Slogan of Vichy France, 1940–4.

14 Mexican version of 'Yankee Go Home', widely used throughout Latin America from 1950 on, protesting against US military and business presence.

A DIAMOND IS FOREVER

It is odd, at first glance, that diamonds should need advertising. Are they not their own best advertisement? But in 1939 the South Africa-based De Beers Consolidated Mines launched a campaign to promote further the diamond engagement ring tradition. It was devised by the N. W. Ayer agency of Chicago and the original copy was written by B. J. Kidd. The idea was not new. Anita Loos in her novel *Gentlemen Prefer Blondes* (1925) enshrined it in: 'Kissing your hand may make you feel very, very good but a diamond and safire bracelet lasts for ever.' Ian Fleming gave a variation of the phrase as the title of his 1956 James Bond novel *Diamonds Are Forever*. Technically speaking, however, diamonds are not forever. It takes a high temperature, but, being of pure carbon, they will burn.

YOU KNOW IT MAKES SENSE

The voice of officialdom in the UK as reflected in cajoling slogans:

Clunk, Click, Every Trip The sound of a car door closing and seat-belt being fastened, used in road safety ads featuring Jimmy Savile from 1971.

Don't Ask A Man To Drink And Drive First used 1964.

Dull It Isn't Metropolitan Police, 1972. The day after the brief TV and poster campaign using this slogan started, it was apparent that the phrase was catching on. A young policeman went to break up a fight at White Hart Lane football ground. Having seized a young hooligan, the constable emerged, dishevelled but triumphant, from the mêlée. A voice from the crowd cried out: 'Dull it effing isn't, eh?'

It's A Man's Life Army recruitment, quoted 1963.

Join The Army And See The World Current 1920s and 1930s. (Eric Partridge gives the response 'Join the Army and see the world – the next one!' as c. 1948.) (Compare: 'I joined the Navy to see the world. And what did I see? I saw the sea.')

Join The Professionals Regular army recruitment campaign, current 1968. The phrase emerged from extensive research which showed that it 'encapsulated all that young men who were in the target range most admired'.

Keep Britain Tidy The simplest of messages and one of the most enduring. Promoted through the Central Office of Information (as were most of these slogans), it first appears in their records as a sticker produced for the Ministry of Housing and Local Government in 1952. However, it was probably coined around 1949. Two years before *that*, the word 'litterbug' was coined for use by the New York City Department of Sanitation.

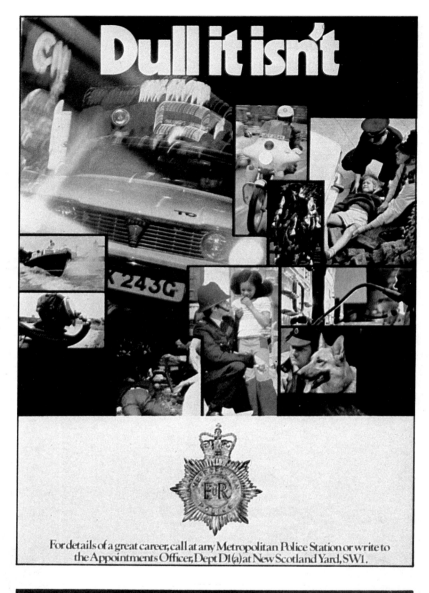

KEEP DEATH OFF THE ROAD

CARELESSNESS KILLS

Keep Death Off The Road (Carelessness Kills) Nobody knows who created this message – the best known of any used in government-sponsored advertising campaigns through the COI. It was used in the memorable poster by W. Little, featuring the so-called 'Black Widow', in 1946.

Save It Energy conservation campaigns from April 1975 to May 1979 used this phrase – on behalf of the government's Department of Energy. Specifically, during the long, dry summer of 1976, it was applied to conservation of water supplies. (Variations have included **Turn It Off** and the informal **Save Water – Bath With A Friend**.)

Watch Out, There's A Thief About Home Office crime prevention campaigns run by the COI first used this slogan *c*. 1966.

Would You Be More Careful If It Was You Who Got Pregnant? Quoted 1978. Headline of a Health Education Council poster showing a pregnant male.

You Know It Makes Sense The pay-off line to all road safety campaigns from 1968 to 1970; not so much a slogan as a summing-up of all the different road safety campaigns. However, the phrase was used with emphasis on the BBC TV programme *That Was The Week That Was* in 1963 which suggests that it was current before this.

YOU, TOO, CAN HAVE A BODY

Taking care of yourself – inside and out:

Acts Twice As Fast As Aspirin   Bufferin; US, current 1951.

All Over The World Good Mornings Begin With Gillette   Gillette razor blades; UK, current c. 1952.

Avoid Five O'Clock Shadow   Gem razors and blades; US, current 1945.

Be Careful How You Use It   Hai Karate deodorant; US, quoted 1979.

Because You Are The Very Air He Breathes   Veto deodorant; US, quoted 1958. Norman B. Norman of the Norman, Craig, Kummel agency asks: 'Why advertise what everybody expects? Of course it should stop perspiration, people expect that. We gave them a slogan with empathy, that gets at the very heart of the matter.'

"I know we're becalmed but there must be something we can do – now that you're rid of your '5 o'clock Shadow'."

BE PREPARED!

Gem Blades are made by the makers of your Gem Razor. They fit precisely. This famous combination positively prevents "5 o'clock Shadow"; it's the last word in shaving comfort. Always use a Gem Blade in your Gem Razor!

AVOID '5 O'CLOCK SHADOW' WITH

GEM RAZORS and BLADES

KEEP YOUR EYE ON THE INFANTRY— The Doughboys are on the job!

Bufferin

TRADE-MARK

Acts twice as fast as aspirin!

Dr Williams' Pink Pills For Pale People UK, current 1900. 'The artful alliteration ... may have done much to build up the £1,111,000 fortune which George Taylor Fulford acquired from this property.' (Turner)

Every Picture Tells A Story Sloane's Backache and Kidney Pills; UK, current 1907. The picture showed a person bent over with pain.

First Thing Every Morning Renew Your Health With ENO's Eno's fruit salts laxative; UK, current 1927.

Helps The Plain, Improves The Fair Pomeroy Face Cream; UK, quoted 1925.

Helps You Break The Laxative Habit Carter's Little Liver Pills; US, quoted 1958.

I Can't Believe I Ate The Whole Thing Alka-Seltzer; US, from 1972. Howie Cohen and Bob Pasqualine of Wells, Rich, Greene created two extraordinary lines on the 'morning after' theme for Alka-Seltzer. 'I Can't Believe ...' featured in a memorable TV ad delineating the agonies of overindulgence, as did **Try It, You'll Like It**. Both these phrases entered the language, especially the latter, which was used by every comic, every mother, and certainly every waiter in the US for the entire year of the campaign (1971).

Inner Cleanliness Andrews Liver Salts (laxative); UK, current from 1950s. 'To complete your inner cleanliness, Andrews cleans the bowels. It sweeps away troublemaking poisons, relieves constipation, and purifies the blood ...' An earlier generation of Andrews ads featured a man searching through his suitcase and saying **I Must Have Left It Behind**.

Keep 'Regular' With Ex-Lax Ex-Lax chocolate laxative; US, current 1934. Also **When Nature Forgets – Remember Ex-Lax**.

Life. Be In It Health campaign; Australia, from 1975. The Department of Youth, Sport and Recreation in the State of Victoria initiated a campaign to get people off their backsides and join in sports. Amid debate as to its worth, the slogan was taken up nationally and the Federal Government declared 2 December as 'Life. Be In It' day. Rejoinders include 'Life. Be Out Of It' and (from Barry Humphries) 'Life. Be Up It'.

Make Your Armpit Your Charm Pit Stopette spray deodorant: US, current early 1950s.

Mennen For Men   The Mennen Company's talcum powder; US, current 1941. Obvious play on words designed to overcome male resistance to using the product.

Nothing Acts Faster Than Anadin   Anadin analgesic tablets; UK, current from 1960s. (It inspired the graffiti retort: 'Then why not use Nothing?') From earlier TV ads: 'Headache? Tense, nervous headache? Take Anadin.'

Often A Bridesmaid, But Never A Bride   Listerine mouthwash; US, from *c.* 1923. One of the best known lines in advertising, written by Milton Feasley of Lambert & Feasley, though there is an echo of the British music-hall song 'Why am I always a bridesmaid?', made famous by Lily Morris. Also **Her Honeymoon – And It Should Have Been Mine!/Even Your Best Friends Won't Tell You/The Taste You Love To Hate (Twice A Day)**.

Phyllosan Fortifies The Over-Forties   Phyllosan tonic; UK, quoted 1974. (We can hear an echo in the BBC saying: 'Radio 4 over-fortifies the over-forties.')

One Degree Under   Aspro headache pills; UK, current 1960s.

The Priceless Ingredient Of Every Product Is The Honor And Integrity Of Its Maker   Squibb drug products; US, from 1921. Before that year, 'Squibb had never advertised to the public ... the problem given to Raymond Rubicam, then a writer at N. W. Ayer & Son, was to produce a series of advertisements which would sell Squibb to the public and not offend the publicity sensitive medical profession ... One night at two in the morning he seemed as far away from the solution as ever. Wearily gathering up his yellow sheets before going to bed, he took one more look through the mass of headlines he had written. "Suddenly," he writes, "two separate word combinations popped out at me from two different headlines. One was 'The Priceless Ingredient' and the other 'Honor and Integrity'. Instantly, the two came together in my mind ..." The phrase became a permanent part of Squibb advertising.' (Watkins). 'Raymond Rubicam's famous slogan ... reminds me of my father's advice: when a company boasts about its integrity, or a woman about her virtue, avoid the former and cultivate the latter.' (Ogilvy). A later slogan was: **For Years We've Been Making Our Products As If Lives Depend On Them**.

Someone Isn't Using Amplex   Amplex (breath purifier); UK, current 1957.

That Kruschen Feeling   Kruschen salts; UK, current 1920s and 1930s. The ads featured an athletic man who attributed all his powers to Kruschen salts.

Things Happen After A Badedas Bath Badedas bath additive;
UK, from 1966. Helicopters land on your lawn, dashing men lurk
beneath your window. But it is an old fantasy: two hundred years
ago a bath additive claimed to be: 'Admirable for those who have
been almost worn out by women and wine ... it will render their
intercourse prolific.'

Stops Halitosis! Listerine mouthwash; US, from 1921. At first,
Listerine was promoted as a 'safe antiseptic' with countless
hygienic uses. Then in 1921 the Lambert Company decided to use a
clinical term for the ordinary unpleasantness known as 'bad breath'
– halitosis. An anxiety was not only stimulated, it was labelled.
Listerine sales climbed from 115,000 a year in 1921 to 4 million a
year in 1927. (Atwan). 'Who can steal "Stops Halitosis" from
Listerine? Dozens of other mouthwashes stop halitosis. Many tried
to move in on this great classic Unique Selling Proposition, until it
became almost a source of embarrassment to them, seeking ways to
phrase their imitation, so that they did not advertise the leader.
This U.S.P., in the public's mind, belongs to Listerine.' (Reeves).
Also **For Halitosis, Use Listerine**.

Within The Curve Of A Woman's Arm Odorono toilet water; US,
from 1919. James Young of J. Walter Thompson wrote the original.
Two hundred *Ladies Home Journal* subscribers cancelled their
subscriptions when the ad tackled 'a frank discussion of a subject
too often avoided', but the deodorant's sales increased by 112 per
cent in that year.

A Fine Cabinet Photograph of President Harrison FREE.

THE GREAT ENGLISH MEDICINE

BEECHAM'S PILLS

PAINLESS (WORTH A GUINEA A BOX) EFFECTUAL

For Bilious and Nervous Disorders, such as Wind and Pain in the Stomach, Sick Headache, Giddiness, Fulness, and Swelling after Meals, Dizziness and Drowsiness, Cold Chills, Flushings of Heat, Loss of Appetite, Shortness of Breath, Costiveness, Scurvy, Blotches on the Skin, Disturbed Sleep, Frightful Dreams, and all Nervous and Trembling Sensations, &c. THE FIRST DOSE WILL GIVE RELIEF IN TWENTY MINUTES. This is no fiction. Every sufferer is earnestly invited to try one Box of these Pills, and they will be acknowledged to be a Wonderful Medicine.
BEECHAM'S PILLS, taken as directed, will quickly restore females to complete health. For a

WEAK STOMACH, IMPAIRED DIGESTION, DISORDERED LIVER,

they ACT LIKE MAGIC. A few doses will work wonders upon the Vital Organs, strengthening the muscular System, restoring long-lost Complexion, bringing back the keen edge of appetite, and arousing with the ROSEBUD OF HEALTH the whole physical energy of the human frame. These are "facts" admitted by thousands, in all classes of society; and one of the best guarantees to the nervous and debilitated is that BEECHAM'S PILLS HAVE THE LARGEST SALE OF ANY PATENT MEDICINE IN THE WORLD. Full directions with each box. Prepared only by
THOS. BEECHAM, St. Helens, Lancashire, England.
Sold by druggists generally. B. F. ALLEN & CO., 365 and 367 Canal Street, New York, Sole Agents for the United States, *who* (if your druggist does not keep them):—inquire first)

A fine full-size Cabinet Photograph of *President Harrison*, will be sent to any one ordering a box of Beecham's Pills, by inclosure of postal note, stamps or cash, to B. F. Allen & Co., Sole Agents for the United States, 365 Canal Street, N. Y., and mentioning THE YOUTH'S COMPANION.

WILL MAIL BEECHAM'S PILLS ON RECEIPT OF PRICE, 25 CENTS A BOX.

Worth A Guinea A Box Beecham's pills; UK, from 1859. This slogan appeared in the first advertisement Thomas Beecham ever placed in a newspaper, the *St Helens Intelligencer*, on 6 August 1859. Family tradition had it that the saying was inspired by a woman in St Helens market who approached Thomas and asked for another box, saying: 'They're worth a guinea to me, lad.' But in 1897 Thomas stated categorically that he had struck out from the metal anvil 'that spark of wit which has made the pills a household word in every quarter of the globe'. A probably apocryphal story has it that an ad was inserted in a church hymnal which led a congregation one day to chorus:

Hark, the Herald Angels sing
Beecham's Pills are just the thing.
For easing pain and mothers mild,
Two for adults, one for a child.

You Too Can Have A Body Like Mine Charles Atlas body-building courses; US, current from 1930s. 'Charles Atlas' was born Angelo Siciliano in Italy in 1894. In his youth he actually was 'a skinny, timid weakling of only seven stone', as the later ads said. 'I didn't know what real health and strength were. I was afraid to fight – ashamed to be seen in a bathing costume.' After watching a lion rippling its muscles at the zoo he developed a method of pitting one muscle against another which he later called **Dynamic Tension**. In 1922 he won the title of **The World's Most Perfectly Developed Man** in a contest sponsored by Bernarr Macfadden and his *Physical Culture* magazine. He started giving mail-order lessons: 'Hey! Quit kicking that sand in our faces!' He died in 1972.

YOURS TO ENJOY IN THE PRIVACY OF YOUR OWN HOME

It takes a dirty mind to know one. But sex sells – or at least that is the conventional wisdom. No amount of protest from the women's movement can prevent some leggy model being stuck on the front of a combine harvester to advertise her charms, if not those of the product. Verbally, too, sex is thrown in to nudge you along – sometimes with quite shameless audacity:

Howard Makes Clothes For Men Who Make Babies

Make-Up To Make Love In
Mary Quant

Are You Getting It Every Day?
Sun newspaper

Give Him A Right Good Hemeling Tonight

Wouldn't You Rather Be Hemeling?
Hemeling beer

That Gleam Is Back In George's Eye Again
Serta Perfect Sleeper mattress

After The Pill: Posturpedic
Sealy mattress

When Should A Blonde Give In?
Clairol

You Know What Comes Between Me And My Calvins? Nothing!
Brooke Shields in Calvin Klein jeans ad, 1980

My Men Wear English Leather Or They Wear Nothing At All

Get Into Fellas
Fellas men's underwear (New Zealand)

A Buck Well Spent On A Spring-Maid Sheet

Is Your Man Getting Enough?
Milk Marketing Board (UK)

Is Your Wife Cold?
National Oil Fuel Institute (US)

Kayser Is Marvelous In Bed

What Makes A Shy Girl Get Intimate?

When A Chic Woman Undresses, What Do You See?

Perhaps We Could, Paul. If ... You Owned A Chrysler

What's The Difference Between A Male Policeman And A Female Policeman? Six Inches
Police recruiting, UK

The First Time Is Never The Best
Campari, US

ACKNOWLEDGEMENTS

Many people have helped me with my inquiries, on both sides of the Atlantic, and I am much indebted to them. My wife, Sue Bates, helped compile the original list of slogans. Helpful suggestions came from Ron and Pat Lehrman, Keith and Avril Ravenscroft, and especially Barry Day, President of McCann & Company. Among the other individuals from advertising agencies and elsewhere who provided information were:

Don Arlett; John Bessant (Central Office of Information); Paul Best; Tony Brignull; Jill Craigie; Julian Bradley (New Scotland Yard); Maurice Drake; Alan Evans (Birds Eye Wall's Ltd); David Hall (Arthur Guinness Son & Co. (Park Royal) Ltd); Dany Khosrovani; David Kingsley; David Lamb (Rowntree Mackintosh Ltd); Terry Lovelock; Jane Maas; Charles Moss; Chris Munds; David McLaren; E. N. Monahan (Shell UK Oil); Roger Musgrave; John Paine; Valerie Simmonds; David Simpson (Action on Smoking and Health); Maurice Smelt; Edward Taylor; Royston Taylor; Peter Thomson (Advertising Standards Authority); Len Weinreich; Fay Weldon; David White (Start-Rite Shoes Ltd); Lois Wyse.

I am also most grateful to many companies and organisations for providing me with research facilities. Among them:

Austin Reed Ltd; Bass Ltd; Bovril Ltd; British Rail; Carnation Foods Company Ltd; Design & Art Directors Association of London; Hoover Historical Center; John Haig & Co. Ltd; John Lewis Partnership Ltd; John Player & Sons Ltd; Leo Burnett USA; Hovis Ltd; Institute of Practitioners in Advertising; Kentucky Fried Chicken (Great Britain) Ltd; Mars Ltd; R. Paterson & Sons Ltd; A. & F. Pears Ltd; Prudential Assurance Company Ltd; RHM Foods Ltd; Jos. Schlitz Brewing Company; The J. M. Smucker Company; Tate & Lyle Ltd; Texaco Ltd; Wm Whiteley Ltd; F. W. Woolworth & Company Ltd.

Peter Leek and Eddie Poulton of George Allen & Unwin masterminded production of the book. Pat Hodgson toiled womanfully over the picture research.

To the authors and publishers of the following books (from some of which I have quoted or reproduced illustrations) my thanks are due:

Atwan/McQuade/Wright, *Edsels, Luckies & Frigidaires* (Dell, 1979). Baglee, Christopher, and Morley, Andrew, *Street Jewellery: A History of Enamel Advertising Signs* (New Cavendish Books, 1978).

Baker, Samm Sinclair, *The Permissible Lie* (Peter Owen, 1969).

Boorstin, Daniel, *The Image* (Weidenfeld & Nicolson, 1960).

Calder, Angus, *The People's War* (Cape, 1969).

Day, Barry (ed.), *100 Great Advertisements* (Times Newspapers, Mirror Group Newspapers, Campaign, 1978).

Feiling, Keith, *The Life of Neville Chamberlain* (Macmillan, 1946).

Flexner, Stuart Berg, *I Hear America Talking* (Simon & Schuster, 1979).

Gable, Jo, *The Tuppenny Punch and Judy Show* (Michael Joseph, 1980).

Hadley, Peter (compiler), *The History of Bovril Advertising* (Bovril, 1970).

Howard, Anthony, and West, Richard, *The Making of the Prime Minister* (Jonathan Cape, 1965).

Jones, Edgar R., *Those Were the Good Old Days* (Simon & Schuster, 1979).

Kleinman, Philip, *Advertising Inside Out* (W. H. Allen, 1977).

Lambert, I. E., *The Public Accepts* (University of New Mexico Press, 1941).

Longmate, Norman, *How We Lived Then* (Arrow, 1973).

Louis, J. C., and Yazijian, Harvey, *The Cola Wars* (Everest House, 1980).

McLaine, Ian, *Ministry of Morale* (George Allen & Unwin, 1979).

Mayer, Martin, *Madison Avenue, USA* (Weidenfeld & Nicolson, 1971).

Nicholl, David Shelley, *Advertising: its Purpose, Principles and Practice* (Macdonald & Evans, 1978).

Ogilvy, David, *Confessions of an Advertising Man* (Atheneum, 1980).

Partridge, Eric, *Dictionary of Slang and Unconventional English* (Routledge & Kegan Paul, 1970).

Partridge, Eric, *Dictionary of Catch Phrases* (Routledge & Kegan Paul, 1977).

Polykoff, Shirley, *Does She ... Or Doesn't She?* (Doubleday, 1975).

Pearson, John, and Turner, Graham, *The Persuasion Industry* (Eyre & Spottiswoode, 1965).

Safire, William, *Safire's Political Dictionary* (Ballantine, 1980).

Sayers, Dorothy L., *Murder Must Advertise* (Gollancz, 1933).

Stiling, Marjorie, *Famous Brand Names, Emblems and Trade Marks* (David & Charles, 1980).

Turner, E. S., *The Shocking History of Advertising* (Michael Joseph, 1952).

Watkins, Julian Lewis, *The 100 Greatest Advertisements* (Dover, 1959).

White, Theodore H., *The Making of the President 1961/1964/1968/1972* (Jonathan Cape, 1962, 1965, 1969, 1973).

Yanker, Gary, *Prop Art* (Darrien House, 1972/Studio Vista, 1972).

PICTURE CREDITS

Cartoons by Bob Warburton.

KEY

GOD   *Those Were the Good Old Days*
100 GA (Watkins)   *The 100 Greatest Advertisements*
ELF   *Edsels, Luckies & Frigidaires*

For full details of these books and of *I Hear America Talking*, *The Persuasion Industry*, *Prop Art* and *Street Jewellery*, see Acknowledgements.

INDEX OF SLOGANS

In addition to slogans, the Index includes the names of people and products frequently mentioned.